NOW THAT I'M STILL HERE

A Memoir of Ruin and Resurrection

CHRISTOPHER J. CARAZAS

Now That I'm Still Here

Copyright © 2025 Christopher J. Carazas

Library of Congress Control Number: 2025916597

ISBN (Hardcover): 979-8-218-75064-0

ISBN (Paperback): 979-8-218-76118-9

ISBN (eBook): 979-8-218-75486-0

Cover design by Christopher J. Carazas

Interior editing by Yvette Nasser

Published by Sentinel House Press

www.sentinelhousepress.com

First Edition

Printed in the United States of America

❀ Formatted with Vellum

WHAT THIS BOOK LEFT BEHIND

"I didn't think a memoir could feel like a mirror. I'm 20. Autistic. Masking every day just to pass. This book didn't just make me cry—it made me *breathe differently.* That matters."
— **Kelsey M.**

"Most memoirs about trauma blink. This one doesn't. It stares directly into the silence that follows collapse and names what lives there. As a therapist, I'll be recommending this for years."
— **Dr. Jenna R.**

"My son didn't survive. I read this with a hand over my mouth. It gave me language for the ache I couldn't name. I saw what I never got to ask."
— **Amanda T.**

"Carazas writes like a man digging through ruins—with poetry, precision, and a quiet fury. *Now That I'm Still Here* is not just beautifully written—it's *necessary literature.*"
— **Simon Li**

"This book cracked something open. It speaks the language of sensory overload, of trying to be 'normal' until your soul splits. I didn't just feel seen—I felt *resurrected.*"
— **Jaya C.**

"Writing trauma is a sacred risk. Carazas doesn't flinch. He walks us through the fire without asking for pity—and what's left is something luminous. This is memoir at its bravest."

— **Elijah R.**

"I've never gone through what he has. But this book made me feel like I had. That's how honest it is. That's how human it is. I held my breath and kept turning pages."

— **Trina K.**

"This isn't about sexuality. It's about survival. About what happens when you shrink to be loved—and how you claw your way back to your full height. It broke me open in the best way."

— **Marcus R.**

"This book should be required reading for anyone who works with neurodivergent kids. It doesn't just explain masking—it *shows* the cost. And it made me want to do better."

— **Rachel K.**

"I grew up swallowing shame and calling it obedience. This book helped me tear that script apart. It's not anti-faith—it's a reclaiming."

— **Lila W.**

"I didn't expect to survive this year. But this book met me where I was—half breathing, half gone—and didn't let go. I'm still here. And maybe, for today, that's enough."

— **Anonymous**

CONTENT NOTE

This book contains depictions of emotional abuse, suicidal ideation, psychiatric hospitalization, and the long, uneven road of healing. It doesn't dwell in graphic detail, but it tells the truth.

Please take care while reading. Step away if you need to. Come back only when your breath feels like yours again. Your safety matters more than the shape of this story. You matter more than any sentence in this book.

If you carry similar wounds, I hope these pages offer you breath, recognition, or even just the reminder that you're not the only one who walked into the dark and lived.

If your path looks different, I hope this story helps you hold space for someone who is still learning how to stay.

If you need support please reach out to:

- **988 Suicide & Crisis Lifeline** (U.S.): Call or text **988**
- **Crisis Text Line**: Text **HELLO** to **741741**
- **International resources**: www.opencounseling.com/suicide-hotlines

You are still here. That means something. Maybe everything.

AUTHOR'S NOTE

This memoir doesn't move in straight lines—and that's on purpose. It coils, fractures, doubles back on itself, because healing does too. It's built from my lived bones, remembered through my flawed, human lens. Memory slips, distorts, forgets —but the moments, the ache, the scars are real. Some names have been changed. This isn't an indictment. It's a survival chant. I've tried to tell the truth as I carried it—raw, trembling, with as much honesty and haunted care as I could hold. If you find yourself here, know this: we don't all survive the same story the same way. This is just how I crawled my way out of mine.

CONTENTS

PROLOGUE

The Quiet After the Storm

THE QUIET LIED. It looked like stillness. It felt like aftermath.

Not the comforting kind of quiet. The other kind. The kind that settles like ash. That buzzes in your ears like something just ended, but no one told your body. Like a verdict, whispered.

It was the start of April 2025. I woke up surrounded by beeping ghosts and the aftertaste of antifreeze.

My apartment creaked with a kind of stillness that made me feel like a trespasser in my own life. My German Shepherd lay beside me, twitching in sleep. The fridge buzzed like it had been holding itself together too long—like me.

The clock on the wall ticked with surgical precision, like it was counting down to something I hadn't agreed to. And the wind wouldn't stop pressing against the glass, like it knew I was cracked.

I didn't move.

I didn't cry.

I just sat in the dark and listened to my chest and tried to decide if the weight in it meant I was alive or not. My phone buzzed once. I didn't check it. The notification sat like a ghost on the screen.

At the same time a year earlier, I was in a psych ward.

That place isn't a sanctuary. It's a waiting room for people the world has run out of answers for. You count ceiling tiles because they're the only things that don't change.

You learn which nurses bark and which ones weaponize warmth. You memorize the schedule, because unpredictability feels like violence.

You smile when they ask questions because the right smile gets you out faster. You learn to survive systems built to contain pain, not heal it.

There was a kid across the hall who screamed in Morse code. Three short, three long, three short. I don't know if he meant SOS, but I counted each sound like it was my own pulse. I never learned his name.

Six months before that, I was married to someone who weaponized concern. No yelling. Just precise cuts disguised as clarity.

"You're too much."

"You don't know how to function."

"You should be grateful I put up with you."

She didn't scream. She didn't need to. Her voice got inside my wiring.

I once told her I was proud of something I'd written. She said, "You should write that down before you fall apart again."

She said my autism made me unlovable. And I believed her.

You don't just walk away from that kind of damage. You carry it. You wear it. It becomes your inner narrator. The one that whispers at parties. The one that edits your texts. The one that makes you feel like every room you walk into was fine until you got there.

But it didn't start there.

In 1989, while living in Bolivia, I once stuck a key into a socket because someone changed the wallpaper pattern. I was four.

I screamed when the electricity hit, but not from pain—from

chaos. From the disruption of ritual. They called it a tantrum. I called it terror. That was the first time silence felt like safety.

But this wasn't a story I ever intended to tell. Not like this. Not for you. Not for anyone.

This was meant to stay buried. Left in the basement with the bottle I almost finished drinking. Filed away under "too messy to explain."

I didn't want to write this. Because writing it meant remembering. And remembering meant reliving the slow unraveling—the way shame moved in and made a home behind my ribs.

Shame that I'm autistic. That I have to rehearse what comes naturally to others. That I second-guess every interaction until it echoes.

Shame that I stayed in a marriage where silence was a weapon, and I let myself be erased, inch by inch, until I forgot what my voice sounded like uncorrected.

That kind of abuse—the slow kind, the kind that recalibrates your worth—it doesn't just break you. It rewrites you.

I stopped trusting people. Stopped answering honestly. I started pretending I was okay because it felt safer than being real and abandoned for it.

Eventually, I convinced myself this was how it would be.

That nothing would ever feel whole again. That I'd walk through the rest of my life like a ghost in my own story.

I'm not religious, but there's that saying: When you plan, God laughs.

Then came Ava.

You'll meet her. Eventually.

She didn't knock. She just arrived—like breath after too long underwater.

She looked straight at me, not through me.

Not around me, but at me. And somehow, she didn't flinch.

But I did.

Because part of me wanted to be loved. And the rest of me

only saw alarms. Red flags that weren't hers but looked just close enough to feel dangerous.

So I sabotaged.

Quietly.

Gently.

The way trauma teaches you to.

I kept her at arm's length and then ached that she didn't feel close.

Then she got sick.

Hospital. IVs. Monitors. Sterile quiet.

The kind of quiet that buzzes, not so different from the one I'd crawled out of. And I thought, "She's going to need something to hold on to."

So, I opened a document. And I wrote.

Not for healing.

Not for publication.

For her.

Something to read to her. Something that explained why I'd been clawing so hard to be loved by someone who already loved me.

It was a confession. It was a breadcrumb trail back to the parts of me I'd abandoned. It was hers.

She never got to hear her chapter. And that sentence has never stopped echoing. But something happened in the writing. Something sacred.

I felt breath again. Like the tiniest opening. Like the air in the room had shifted. Not warmer, not lighter, just possible.

And I wondered, maybe this isn't just for her. Maybe it's for someone else too. Someone like you.

Someone who's been bent under the weight of someone else's version of love. Someone who's memorized the silence between insults and still called it peace. Someone whose voice was turned against them so many times, they stopped using it altogether.

So, I kept writing. For you.

Not to offer answers, but to name the ache.

Not to heal you, but to let you know you're not walking through this haunted house alone.

That healing is not linear. It doesn't ascend like a movie montage. It doubles back. It hides. It knocks the breath out of you, then disappears.

So if this story feels disjointed at times, that's because it is.

So was I. It will loop. It will fracture. It will forget itself and return.

But stay with it. Stay with me. Eventually, it clicks. Like breath. Like silence broken. Like love—when you finally believe you deserve it.

This book isn't about healing. Not the kind you hashtag. Not the kind you put under a sunrise caption.

It's about what comes before that. It's about standing in a basement with a bottle of antifreeze and not knowing if you want to die, just knowing you don't want to be anymore. It's about unscrewing the cap and wondering if this counts as suicide or just surrender. It's about holding on because of a dog upstairs who still expects you to come back.

Her name is Shadow. I got her in Madagascar. She has seen more than most people. She has curled beside me in every storm I couldn't name. She waited outside every door I locked behind myself. When I wanted to die, she scratched at the frame like she knew. Like she refused to let go.

Because of her, I walked. Because of her, I spoke. Because of her, I survived.

This book is about the silence after the scream. When nothing moves. When the echo clears. And you realize you're still breathing.

It's about how, somehow, love showed up with Ava, four months after Marianne disappeared from my doorway. Only two months after I staggered out of the ward still shaking.

Before I earned it.

Before I was ready for anything.

Before I believed I could hold something tender without shattering it.

And she didn't flinch.

Not once.

Not even when I did.

She sat next to me once and didn't say a word. Just reached out, touched my hand, and didn't pull back. I kept waiting for the judgment. For the shift in her eyes. It never came. She stayed. Like stillness. Like clarity.

So no, this isn't a hero story. It's not a comeback arc.

It's a record of survival. Of slow, stubborn breathing. Of learning to exist again after your own voice was turned against you.

If you've ever stood in the doorway of your own life and thought, they'd be better off without me. If your name feels too heavy in your mouth, if your skin feels more like a wall than a home. This book is for you.

I didn't die. I didn't disappear.

But more than that, I clawed my way back. Inch by inch. Breath by breath. Some days I still do.

I showed up to the stillness. I stared down the silence. I stayed.

And maybe that's not a miracle. Maybe that's not something that gets quoted under a sunset photo.

But it's mine. It's survival. It's breath I wasn't supposed to take and I took it anyway.

If you're still breathing too—scarred, shaky, unsure—then maybe that counts for something.

No. Not maybe. It counts for everything.

Even if no one claps.

Even if no one sees.

Especially then.

Part One

THE MASK AND THE MYTH

First, we learned to smile without blinking.
Then we learned to disappear while staying in the room.
The mask didn't hide us. It hollowed us.
And the applause was louder than the screaming.
No one saw the fracture.
Because we made it look like grace.

1

THE LIE OF WORTHLESSNESS

Every story has a cursed object. Mine was a voice.

"YOU KNOW, you're exhausting to be around." I don't remember what I said before that. Just the shape of her back as she faced the sink. The sponge moved in slow circles. The clink of ceramic against ceramic. The hum of the fridge like a warning tone. She didn't look at me when she said it.

Flat. Neutral. Like she was noting the weather.

That's how it usually was. Never screaming. No insults hurled across a room. Just low-volume dismantling. Soft-spoken demolition.

I remember standing there frozen, thinking absurdly about how her ponytail hung slightly to the left. As if the asymmetry of her hair mattered more than the sentence that had just shattered me.

The first time she said it, it cut deep. The tenth time, I thought: maybe I am.

That's how it happens.

You start out defending yourself. "I didn't mean it like that."

"I'm trying." "I'm sorry." Eventually you stop. Not because you believe you're wrong, but because you get tired of hearing your own voice sound so desperate.

And if you're autistic — if you've spent your whole life being too much for people — you start to think maybe she's just saying what everyone else has been too polite to admit.

She was good at that. Framing her cruelty as honesty. Like the time I told her I was overwhelmed after a rough day, and she smiled and said, "You always make everything harder than it needs to be." She said it like she was helping me see something I couldn't, like she was doing me a favor. And for a moment, I believed her.

She'd say things like, "I don't know how people put up with you," or "You're just a lot." And then she'd laugh. Like it was a joke. Like I was supposed to laugh too.

So, I did. Because if I laughed first, maybe it wouldn't sting as much. If I made myself the punchline, maybe she'd stop aiming for the heart.

You fold. You apologize for things that aren't wrong. You shrink in small, almost invisible ways. You mistake survival for maturity.

I started editing myself, toning down the way I talked about the things I loved, like the obscure history podcasts I used to ramble about, or the music I'd write at night that never felt worth sharing anymore. I paused before I said anything that might be too intense. I tried to package myself into something quieter, simpler, less... me.

Even that wasn't enough.

I remember brushing my teeth one night. I looked up, caught my reflection, and thought not even dramatically, just matter of fact, "God, I must be impossible to live with."

It didn't sound like her voice anymore. It sounded like mine.

That's when you know the lie has sunk its teeth in—not when they say it, but when *you* do. When it slides out of your mouth without thought, smooth, rehearsed, leaving no ripple in your chest.

The worst part isn't their voices echoing in your memory; it's your own voice, gentle and cruel all at once, threading itself through your thoughts like mold creeping along damp walls, patient as plague. It's not loud. Not even fully formed. Just there, soft, invasive, staining everything. A lens you didn't ask for, a film over your eyes, so every thought passes through it first, strained like water through a rag steeped in rot.

And then the chorus begins, quiet and familiar:

"Don't say that."

"It's weird."

"You're too much—again."

"They're only smiling because they pity you."

"God. Shut up. Please, just shut up."

It gets quieter over time, but sharper. Less like someone yelling at you, more like your own conscience keeping you in line.

I'd reread every text five times before sending them. I'd delete entire messages because they felt too long, too honest, too...me.

And I'd convince myself that was emotional intelligence. Awareness. Maturity. It wasn't. It was fear dressed up like wisdom.

Sometimes, I'd walk into a room and immediately scan for what part of me didn't belong. Was I too loud? Too quiet? Too awkward? Was my face giving away too much? Was I forgetting some invisible social rule everyone else understood instinctively?

And I'd hear it, the voice of the Dark Passenger:

"You're exhausting."

"People are just being nice."

"They don't really like you."

"You're the weird one. Always have been."

I thought I was getting better. Thought I was becoming

easier to love. Because I didn't argue. I didn't take up space. I stopped asking for anything.

But I wasn't getting better. I was disappearing.

I carried that lie with me long after she was gone. Into new and existing connections. Into silence. Even into love.

Because when someone was kind to me, I didn't know what to do with it. I'd question it. Twist it. Assume there was some angle I hadn't seen yet.

I became suspicious of gentleness. Uncomfortable with patience. If someone said I mattered, I'd smile and thank them, but inside, I was already poking holes in it.

They don't know the full story. They're just being nice. They'll leave eventually. Everyone does.

Then in late June of 2024, I started falling for someone again. Ava.

It terrified me. Not because I didn't feel it, but because she was the first to offer me kindness without a hook buried beneath it.

She'd look at me like I was worth something. Like I was good.

And every time, it felt like standing under a light I didn't earn.

Kindness was foreign to me. It hummed with danger.

I kept waiting for the moment it would turn — teeth bared, ledger open.

I couldn't hold her gaze without feeling counterfeit, already bracing for the verdict. Already practicing my apology for being exactly who I am.

Sometimes Ava would ask, "Are you okay?" And I'd smile. Lie. Change the subject. Because how do you confess that the man you're trying to become is still duct-taped with the voice that almost ended him?

That you don't trust love because love, before, came with conditions, clauses, and consequences?

That being seen doesn't feel like freedom, it feels like exposure?

That's the cost of believing you're worthless. Even when people try to love you, you're never quite sure they should.

That love, even her soft kind, felt like a weapon waiting to break skin.

Because before, love always came with claws.

Clauses.

Consequences.

Being seen didn't feel like freedom.

It felt like exposure. Like standing on a pier waiting for the match.

That's what believing you're worthless does to you.

Even when someone tries to love you, you're never sure they should.

Ava was the first kindness I ever flinched from. I wish I could tell you how I bled from it.

THE CURSED OBJECT

It doesn't look dangerous.
That's how it gets you.
It sounds like someone you loved once.
And all it says is: "They were right about you."
It was my voice.

The basement was colder than I expected. The kind of cold that makes air feel like it's pressing against your skin. My breath came out in shallow clouds. Every corner of that space held echoes. The hum of the overhead light flickered like it couldn't decide whether to stay on. It didn't feel peaceful. It felt like a verdict.

The bottle was on the shelf. Antifreeze. I don't even remember buying it.

I wasn't crying. Wasn't shaking. Just... still.

The voice in my head wasn't screaming. It was calm. Rational. That's the part people don't get.

"You're tired. You've always been too much."

"She was right."

"No one is built to love you for long. This is mercy. Quiet is better than being a burden."

Another voice stirred. Not hers. Not mine. The Dark Passenger.

"I've been here a long time," it said. *"I was with you in Bolivia. When you bit the neighbor's cow and your father dragged you inside. When you rocked back and forth in school and they laughed. When the teacher said you were 'too intense.'"*

"I'm not a scream," it whispered. *"I'm a whisper with perfect timing."*

"I'm what protects you from being known. From being abandoned again."

I stared at the bottle and thought how peaceful it would be not to end anything. Just to stop. To vanish. To not be the difficult one anymore. And that didn't scare me. That's what scared me.

Then came the gulp.

And then another.

And another.

No montage.

No divine flash.

There was just the sound of my dog Shadow shifting upstairs. Her paws on the wood floor. Maybe that was enough.

Maybe it wasn't hope that saved me. Maybe it was just something that still expected me to exist. I turned away. Walked back upstairs. Sat on the couch in the dark.

I didn't choose life that night.

It's just that death didn't choose me.

THE WHISPERER

He never raises his voice. He doesn't have to.
He just waits until your own reflection says it first.
Then he nods, satisfied. "See?"

Maybe that's where this story begins. In my apartment in Plymouth in July of 2024. A text from Ava. Unexpected. Six words: "Hey. Just thinking of you today."

No context.

No follow-up.

Just presence.

And it felt... wrong.

My instinct was suspicion. I waited for the real message. But it never came. Instead, I sat with this small, unearned kindness vibrating in my hand.

If they really were thinking of me, just because, then everything I believed about myself would start to crack.

The dark passenger pushed back. *"They're just being polite. They don't know the real you."*

But a smaller voice — one I hadn't heard in years — whispered: *"What if they do? And still care?"*

It didn't feel like comfort. It felt like exposure.

I didn't reply. I just stared at it, unsure which version of myself to believe.

But it was the first time I realized that maybe the problem wasn't that I was too much. Maybe the problem was how small I'd been taught to stay.

The dark passenger still whispers. When I speak too long. When I take up space. When someone's kindness lasts too long and I start bracing for the blow.

"You're too much."

"You're too broken."

"They're going to leave."

But now... I whisper back.

And sometimes... I'm louder.

2

THE BOY BETWEEN WORLDS

I didn't grow up in America. I just landed here and learned to act like I belonged.

THE FIRST THING that struck me about Massachusetts was how quiet the houses were. Not quiet like peace. A quiet like something buried. A silence that didn't breathe. A hush that felt like absence.

My chest tightened in that stillness, like I'd stepped into a world that had forgotten how to exhale.

It was 1997. We had just moved from Ghana. Even there the silence had sound. Jungle insects humming. Dogs barking from distant rooftops. The grind of generators kicking in after another blackout.

But here? Just wind. Asphalt. The occasional car, a slow exhale through clenched teeth. Even the birds seemed unsure they belonged.

The neighborhood looked like it had been vacuum-sealed. Lawns like carpet. Mailboxes like soldiers. Every house identical —like the place had been designed by someone who feared contrast. I remember standing at the edge of our driveway, back-pack heavy, stomach tighter than my shoelaces, and thinking: I didn't know how to exist here.

Other places had a pulse I could slip into—the predictable churn of the expat circuit, the familiar dance of arrivals and departures.

But here? Here the air felt sterilized. Here there was no script for a boy who carried too many languages in his mouth and didn't know which one this silence wanted.

I was fourteen. Starting ninth grade. For the first time, I was living in the country printed on the front of my passport. I should've felt proud.

But instead, I felt counterfeit. Like someone had stamped a label on me that didn't match the contents. I was American. That's what the paperwork said. But paper doesn't bleed.

THE LIE IN THE MIRROR

I was American.
That's what the paper vowed.
But paper doesn't sweat.
Doesn't flinch.
Doesn't whisper to be less. I did.
So, I smiled— like laying a lamb on the altar.
Lied—like it was breath, like it was prayer.
Because here, they only cradle
what stays clean, only praise
what never spills its red
on their precious, holy white.

By then, I'd lived in five countries. Ecuador. Bolivia. Paraguay. Ghana. The U.S. I spoke too many languages. I knew how to leave. How to rebuild. How to disappear. I'd survived schools where your accent was your fingerprint. Where kids moved like satellites—always circling, never landing. Where belonging was borrowed, and the only rule was learn fast or vanish.

Then I landed in a public high school in small-town Massachusetts. Where none of that mattered.

In Accra, the classroom was a constellation. Students from everywhere. Teachers who knew how to pronounce your name without asking twice or making a joke of it. There was a boy from Denmark who taught me to juggle. A girl from Côte d'Ivoire who braided my friend's hair during science.

We passed footballs during breaks and shifted desks mid-year without needing reasons. Everything moved. Everything breathed.

Here, nothing moved. The social lines were etched in concrete. Kids clung to their cliques like lifeboats. They weren't mean. Just uninterested. There was no curiosity—just certainty. Just legacy. Everyone had known each other since they could speak. I was the new kid in a place where new meant defective.

This wasn't just culture shock. This was a language I didn't know how to fake.

And then there was the whiteness. Not just skin—sameness. It was cultural uniformity that pressed in like fog. The cafeteria echoed with one voice, one rhythm, one version of America. If anyone asked where I was from, it was just to set up a punchline.

"Do you ride llamas in Bolivia?"

"Is Ghana in Africa?"

"You speak French? Like, croissant-French?"

I smiled. Always smiled. Because survival, at that age, isn't about honesty. It's about camouflage.

First period, I walked into the wrong classroom—Algebra II instead of Earth Science. I sat down, took out my notebook, tried to look like I belonged.

"Welcome to Algebra II," the teacher said.

Someone laughed. I felt it in my spine.

"Sorry, miss," I said, too politely.

No one said "miss" here. My accent made the word hang like smoke.

I found the right room late. Only one seat left—in front. I

walked past the stares. You know that kind of silence, when it's not quiet, it's watching you?

The teacher circled my name in red. Didn't speak.

Red means wrong. Red means marked.

At lunch, I sat alone. I opened a container of arroz con pollo. Real food. The smell of home—garlic, cumin, memory. Comfort in Tupperware.

Someone wrinkled their nose. "What is that?"

"Chicken and rice," I said, voice small. They laughed. Not cruel. Just careless.

So, I laughed too. Because if you laugh with them, they don't aim it at you.

After lunch, a kid shouted, "Yo! Say something in French!" I said something. They mocked it. Cartoon accent. Laughter again.

Another asked if I'd ridden a llama to school.

I smiled. Always smiled.

That's when the dark passenger stirred again.

"*Blend in*," it whispered. "*You've done it before. You don't belong. So, vanish.*"

In history, the teacher asked about the consequences of colonialism in Africa. I raised my hand. I had lived it. I spoke of borders drawn by outsiders, tribes split apart, languages crushed.

She cut me off. "We're not getting into politics."

Everyone turned. Eyes like gun barrels. The silence turned sharper. The dark passenger coiled tighter.

"*Told you,*" it said. "*They don't want the real you.*"

Last period was gym. Soccer—my safe place. I called it football. They laughed. "Dude, this is America." I nodded like I'd meant it as a joke.

I didn't take the shortcut home. Too many voices. Too many chances to be noticed for the wrong reasons.

That night, my mom asked how school was.

"Fine," I said. My voice was neutral. But my stomach ached from holding in every word I hadn't said.

There was one kid—Alex. Torn hoodie. Hair in his face. Eyes like he didn't care anymore. We were lab partners. I did the work. He copied. It worked.

One day, he passed me a note: "Skating after school. You in?"

I stared at it like it was written in code. My brain flooded with questions: What if I say the wrong thing? What if I wear the wrong clothes? What if I laugh wrong? What if I fall? What if they see me?

"*Don't risk it*," the dark passenger warned. "*You know how this ends*."

I wrote back: "Can't. Family thing."

A lie. Of course it was.

He never asked again.

A week later, a girl looked at me during lunch. Really looked.

"Where are you from?" she asked. No edge. Just curiosity.

I froze. I hesitated. Then started listing: "Bolivia. Senegal. Ghana. Paraguay. And—"

She blinked. "So, like, Army brat?"

"No," I said. Too sharp. Then softer: "I'm just...from everywhere."

She nodded. "Cool." And turned back to her fries.

Maybe, for a second, she saw it—the static behind my eyes. The tension in my jaw. The way I folded my hands to keep from unraveling.

But only for a second.

You don't vanish all at once. You fade. You bleed out in reverse.

I stopped correcting people when they mispronounced my last name. Stopped explaining that I wasn't new to school—I was just new to the country. I stopped being a person. Started becoming a version.

Because no one wants the full story. They just want you to make sense.

So, I did.

I learned the phrases. "Dude." "Whatever." "That's sick."

"Wicked." They tasted wrong. But they worked. Like a passport with someone else's photo.

I watched. I mirrored. I folded.

How they leaned on lockers. How they shouted in class without getting punished. How they chewed gum like rebellion.

It wasn't just the language. It was the rhythm. The choreography of belonging.

Where I came from, you earned your way in. Here, you pretended not to care—and if you were lucky, they let you orbit.

So, I laughed. I nodded. I stopped raising my hand. I stopped bringing food that smelled like anywhere real.

And the boy who had crossed oceans? Who spoke four languages? Who could navigate airports and cultures and power cuts?

He dimmed. Not American. Just...less foreign.

One morning, I looked in the mirror. Hoodie adjusted. Sleeves pulled. Eyes blank. I practiced a "what's up" that didn't sound like an apology. And thought "if I get this right, maybe I won't feel so tired all the time."

But I did. Because being someone else costs more than anyone tells you.

And I was bleeding out in smiles and silence.

Massachusetts was quiet. But inside me, something screamed.

A static I couldn't name. A hunger to belong. A rage with nowhere to go.

THE ECHO IN MY CHEST

It wasn't grief
It wasn't fear.
It was every unspoken scream vibrating through bone.

The boy between worlds was starting to split.

And I didn't yet know how many versions of me I'd have to kill just to survive the next one.

3

THE SKIN I COULDN'T ESCAPE

I didn't know I was wearing a mask until it started to crack.

IT HAPPENED SLOWLY, at first. It began quiet. A subtle wrapping at the edges of my calm. Nothing obvious. Sensory threads pulled tight. Too bright. Too loud. Too close. That's when the panic found the seams in my mask and started to pry.

It was in the locker room, where everything seemed to move in a rhythm I couldn't follow. The mirror was warped, smudged with fingerprints like it didn't want to see me either.

Around me, the other boys were shouting, laughing, their bodies bared without hesitation. Shirts flew off. Deodorant cans hissed as they sprayed their sweat away. One kid flexed in front of the mirror, and another howled with laughter. Their voices ricocheted off the tiles, sharp and loud. Everything about them was easy. The sweat was celebrated. Their bodies felt like home.

But mine? My body felt like a stranger I couldn't outrun. I stood fully clothed, hood up, pretending to dig through my gym bag.

My shoulders tight, my hands shaking, too aware of every

movement, every breath. I couldn't stop myself from feeling it: the panic simmering beneath my skin, tightening like a vise around my chest.

The dark passenger was there, too, in the corner of the room, watching.

There was a day during gym class, dodgeball. I barely moved. I stood frozen at the back of the gym, tracking every throw, my heart thumping in my chest, trying not to flinch.

It was like the air was thick, pressing down on me. The harder I tried not to panic, the worse it got. After class, one of the boys turned to me and said, "You don't sweat, do you? Are you like... a robot or something?"

I laughed. I didn't know how else to respond. The kind of laugh you practice so no one smells the fear underneath. Later that night, I scrubbed my armpits raw, even though I hadn't done anything.

I started wearing hoodies all the time. Even in May. Even when the air felt like it was about to suffocate me. Layers became armor. A barrier between the world and the raw nerve underneath. My body. My skin. Everything about me felt too loud, too wrong.

There were moments when I walked down the hall and couldn't breathe right. My chest would tighten. My vision would blur. I felt like I was walking underwater.

The world would tilt, and everything felt too close. And the passenger would whisper: *"Easy now. Don't break where they can see."*

One time, my voice cracked in class. Just once. The whole room laughed. I didn't speak the rest of the period. I couldn't.

I didn't have the words for it. Dysregulation. Shutdown. Autistic masking. All I knew was this: my body betrayed me. It was loud when I needed to be invisible. It exposed me.

So, I trained it.

Stillness became my gospel. Smiles became currency. I hid my stims (small rituals of the body that kept the panic at bay) inside my sleeves, changed clothes facing the wall, kept my eyes low, my steps even, my tone neutral. I learned to disappear.

But every time I looked in the mirror, the face staring back wasn't mine. It was the mask. The version I thought they wanted to see. I practiced it so many times, it became second nature. But it wasn't real. It was just a mask.

I went to the bathroom between classes, not because it was safe, but because it had a lock.

I could shut the door.

I could be alone.

No one would see me.

No one would know.

I'd lock myself in the stall, sit on the toilet lid with my backpack still on. I'd grip my sleeves, clench my jaw, curl into myself. Trying to breathe. Trying to hold everything together just long enough to get through the next class, the next hour, the next person.

Someone would walk in, slam a stall door, laugh. I wouldn't move. I would just sit there, holding onto stillness, holding onto survival.

Eventually, I'd stand up, look in the mirror, and practice the smile they believed. The one that didn't show the panic. The one that said, I'm fine.

And every nod, every easy shrug in response, was its own kind of confirmation: they saw what they wanted. Not me.

I'd walk out like nothing had happened.

Then came the group project. The two words that made my stomach twist. Not because I couldn't do the work, but because I didn't know how to work with people.

Who do you sit next to?

What's too quiet?

What's too much?

When do you laugh?

When do you speak?

What if they see too much?

The passenger whispered: "*Mirror them. Study their movements. Don't blink too long. Don't show your hands.*"

I watched the group like a code, trying to understand how they moved, how they interacted. I mirrored them. I did my part, spoke my lines, hit every beat.

When it was over, the teacher smiled. "Great job. Clear. Confident. Well-organized."

One of the group members leaned in. "You crushed it." I nodded. Said thanks. Smile. Fist bump. Inside: nothing. Static. Echo.

THE GLASS THAT DOESN'T SHATTER
I cracked in silence.
No shards. No blood.
Just the echo where I used to be.

The passenger grinned.

THE PASSENGER GRINS
Praise tastes like poison when it's meant for the mask.

They weren't praising me. They were praising the mask. The calm, controlled version of me. The one that didn't break. And for a moment, that felt worse than being ignored.

This is how it starts, I thought. They clap. You shrink.

I started saying less. I spoke only when spoken to. I disappeared into the background, and they praised me for it. Teachers called me respectful. My parents said I was calm. A girl once said, "You're kind of mysterious. In a cool way."

They didn't know I was drowning. Trying to hold it together. Trying to survive. Trying to be something I wasn't.

At dinner that night, my mom said, "You've really settled in." I smiled. "Yeah. I'm good."

The next day, I got my report card: "Christopher is focused, respectful, and quiet. A joy to have in class."

That sentence hurt more than any insult. It meant the mask had taken. It meant I had learned to vanish—and no one noticed.

The passenger was pleased. *"You're becoming easier to love,"* it whispered.

And that's when I knew: I had learned how to disappear. And no one missed me.

Not even me.

4

FAITH IN THE FIRE

God didn't find me in a church. He found me in the silence between breakdowns.

I WAS fifteen when we started going to the church in Hopkinton. My mom had found it online—non-denominational, with a youth group that met on Friday nights and a band that actually played music that sounded like it belonged on the radio.

I didn't know what to expect, but I was lonely. I didn't fit in anywhere, so church gave me something to do that didn't require pretending I was fine.

I didn't know what I was looking for. But I knew what I wasn't expecting—warmth. Not the spiritual kind. The human kind. No one stared. No one whispered. No one asked what was wrong with me.

Someone held the door open. Someone smiled and meant it. The smell of burnt coffee and old hymnals. Carpet that muffled everything. The sticky residue of last week's donuts still clinging to the folding chairs.

I had never felt that kind of welcome before. Not in my whole life.

That first night, I sat in the back of the sanctuary, hoodie up, watching the others. I watched them raise their hands during worship, like they were trying to touch something I couldn't see.

The lights were low, the music loud, and the voices blended together, floating upward, lifting as one. I didn't sing. I couldn't. But I watched, studying the way their bodies moved, loose and certain, like they weren't afraid of being seen, of being vulnerable. Like they believed.

That hooked me.

I came back. Then again. Then every week after that.

Eventually, I picked up a guitar. Played a few chords. Then I was on the worship team. Leading songs about surrender, while still learning how to keep my hands from shaking in public.

I sang with my eyes closed, trying to let the music carry me, but it didn't always work. I wasn't sure how to surrender.

There was a boy named Ryan. He gave hugs that cracked your spine, and his laugh came easy, like joy was something you could catch if you were open enough.

Ryan introduced me to everyone. He made space for me without making a show of it, pulling me into his circle like I mattered.

The youth pastor said things like "God's not mad at you" and "You don't have to earn this." No one said I was too much. No one laughed when I talked too fast. They just accepted me.

And when you've spent your whole life feeling like you take up too much space, acceptance feels like salvation.

The church became my lifeline. I joined every trip. Played guitar at every retreat. I led small groups for the younger kids. I learned how to pray out loud without stumbling.

I memorized verses like passwords, like they held the key to something. I threw myself into it, because it felt like I could finally be good at something. Like I could finally fit.

But even then—behind the smiles, the songs, the perfect

Sunday answers—something inside me stayed curled, still, waiting.

The first missions trip I went on was to Spain. We landed in Algeciras. We passed out Bibles to Moroccan migrants who came in and out of the port. I didn't need a translator. I spoke Spanish and French. I was useful. I was safe. I was needed.

But even usefulness can't quiet the dark passenger.

Alejandra was our local contact. I was paired with her for the trip. She was tiny, cute in that effortless way that came from someone who wasn't trying too hard, but her appearance didn't quite prepare you for the power that came with her presence.

Tattoos wrapped around her arms and wrists, a few peeking out from under the sleeves of her black T-shirt. A mix of street smarts and charm, she had this fearless vibe that was contagious.

Despite being only 19, she had a certain kind of toughness that seemed to come naturally—like the streets had shaped her into someone who could navigate any situation, no matter how intense.

She was a paradox: cute, but completely badass. Her voice was soft, but when she spoke, you listened—there was something unshakable in her tone, something that made you want to trust her instantly. Her eyes were sharp, but not cold. They were full of curiosity, warmth, and just the right amount of challenge.

We clicked almost immediately, like we had known each other for years. It was strange—how easy it was to talk to her. It felt like we were old friends, as if we'd been walking the same road for far longer than a couple of days.

The way she made me feel like I wasn't some weird outsider, like I wasn't just another mission to be tolerated—it was refreshing.

Late one night, after the team finished passing out Bibles by the port, we sat on the roof of the church. She lit a cigarette, and the smoke spiraled up into the dark sky, mixing with the city's faint hum below us.

She offered me one, but I declined.

She didn't mind, just took another drag and smiled a little, half amused, half knowing.

I couldn't help but admire her.

"You believe all this?" she asked, her voice low, her words slipping out with a gentle honesty. She didn't say it like a challenge, just an observation, something she was genuinely curious about.

She wasn't the first to ask me that question, but the way she asked it made it feel different.

She wasn't judging me.

She wasn't testing me.

She just wanted to know.

I wasn't sure how to answer. I said I wasn't sure, that I wanted to believe, but it was harder when I was caught up in all the noise—the preaching, the rituals, the songs.

It was easier to believe in the light when you could see it, when it was clear and tangible. But in the dark, it was hard to hold on.

She exhaled a cloud of smoke, looking at me, waiting. Her eyes never left mine.

"Just don't lie to yourself to keep other people comfortable," she said. She didn't offer anything else—just those words, simple but piercing.

It hit me harder than I expected. Her voice was calm, but there was an edge to it, like she'd already learned the hard way that pretending wasn't worth it.

I wanted to respond, to tell her everything, but something held me back.

I wasn't ready to let go of the faith I'd wrapped around myself like a blanket.

THE LIE IN THE MIRROR

Smile like its yours
Lie like its breath.
They only love what they don't have to see.

Alejandra didn't say anything else. She just leaned back against the roof, looking up at the stars, letting the silence settle between us. But I couldn't forget her words. They circled in my head like a quiet storm.

The following summer, we went to Philadelphia. We stayed at a seminary, painting walls, serving meals, praying with the homeless.

I gave my testimony in front of strangers and didn't shake. That was the summer I thought maybe I was healed. Maybe all the broken parts of me had finally fused into something whole.

But by the time I got to college in 2003, it was clear it wasn't that simple.

I went to a Christian college in Illinois.

Rules.

Curfews.

Chapel requirements.

I'd always been a rule follower, so at first, I thought I could make it work. I could fit in. I wanted to go deeper. Serve harder. Be a "light."

By the end of Freshman year, I joined a study abroad program in London, led by a professor everyone loved. He was funny, smart, disarming. He made you feel like you mattered. He made me feel like I was seen.

Until the night he disappeared.

The next morning, we found out he'd been robbed in an alley behind a strip club while receiving a blowjob. The administration said nothing.

No consequences. No acknowledgment.

When I asked why, they told me to be quiet. Told me it wasn't my place.

And just like that, the foundation cracked.

This was the same man who flayed us from pulpits about lust. Who made me shrink from girls like they carried serpents in their pockets. Who would have nailed me to the campus gates for walking on the wrong sidewalk with Eve.

I'd spent months terrified of being expelled for a breath too close, a laugh too late, a smile that wandered. My righteousness was weighed daily in curfews signed, confessions documented, guilt spoon-fed like communion.

But him?

He kept his job. His sermons. His shining halo.

Because he wept, because he *said* he was sorry.

Because repentance, here, was a chalice reserved for the powerful, filled with wine only they were allowed to sip.

It was just another nail in the coffin.

These were the years the Catholic Church was splitting at its stained-glass seams—priests rotated like crops, secrets buried in incense and payoffs, the flock still kneeling with heads bowed under dripping guilt. I used to think that was their sickness, not ours.

But this? This was my altar cracking. My sanctuary spoiled.

THE COVENANT OF SILENCE

We made a pact I never signed.
I give you peace, you give me nothing.
I hide the truth; you build the walls.

If righteousness had loopholes, if truth was optional for the powerful, then what had I been sacrificing for?

The dark passenger stirred.

Told me I was naive.

Told me this was the part where belief unravels.

And maybe it was right.

God didn't leave me that day. But the version of Him they gave me did. And honestly, I haven't missed Him since.

I transferred out of Trinity. I eventually landed at American University in Washington D.C. I didn't leave the faith. Not all at once. But I stopped singing with my eyes closed. I stopped praying out loud. I started noticing the gaps. The performance. The silence around pain.

By the time I graduated from American University in 2009, I still believed in God. But not the church. Not the system that protected the wolves and blamed the wounded.

Still, sometimes I pray.

Not often.

Not publicly.

But when someone I love is slipping through the cracks of this world, I still do it.

Like the day Ava was put on the ventilator.

Like the morning I sat in the ICU parking lot, staring at the blackened sky, asking for something I wasn't sure I believed in to just, please, help her breathe again.

I didn't know, back then in Hopkinton, that someone like Ava would come into my life. But maybe the part of me that kept praying was always waiting for her.

I stopped praying when the script broke. But I never forgot the language.

Maybe that wasn't faith. Maybe it was love in a language I haven't forgotten.

I don't know if I want to go back to Church. But I know there's still a part of me that listens when it's quiet.

And maybe that's enough.

Or maybe it's not.

Somewhere in the static, I could still hear Alejandra's voice: "Don't lie to yourself to keep other people comfortable."

I wasn't ready to let go of faith.

But I had to let go of pretending.

And maybe that was holy too.

5

A FAMILY SHAPED LIKE A FIST

My house was not a war zone, but I still learned how to flinch.

WE DIDN'T YELL, at least not in the way you see on TV, with shattered plates and slammed doors. There were no heated arguments, no screaming matches into the night.

The way my family hurt each other was subtler, quieter. It was in the silences. The way words were measured, portioned out like they were scarce. The way love was doled out in careful doses, rationed like food in wartime.

My father didn't raise his voice. He didn't need to. Disappointment from him was sharp, precise—one look, and it was enough to make the air in the room go cold. His eyes would catch mine, and I'd feel it all—his expectations, his quiet judgment—everything that wasn't said but hung in the space between us.

The silence was worse than any shout.

My mother loved hard, but her love was also wrapped in fear. Fear that I was fragile. That the world would crush me. That I'd get hurt if I moved too fast, too far, too freely.

She was protective, but in a way that felt like restraint, like holding me back instead of giving me room to breathe. She wrapped me in her protection like a blanket, but it was heavy. Too heavy.

When my friends biked to school so we could glide through town afterward, I was told to take the bus. Come home. Stay close. Sleepovers were off-limits; she didn't know their parents, didn't trust their walls to hold me like hers did.

Friday nights became interrogations—who, where, what family? If the answers weren't precise, if they rang wrong in her ears, the night ended in a slammed door and me staring at my bedroom ceiling while laughter floated somewhere beyond reach.

And because of that, they built walls around me, not wings. They wanted to keep me safe from everything, but in doing so, they didn't see what I needed to grow. They didn't see the damage those walls caused.

But they never saw how sometimes safety is just another word for captivity—how soft cages bruise all the same.

No one in my family ever talked about the bite marks I left on the cows in Bolivia, or the way I would rock back and forth on the tile floor when my routine was disrupted.

My family sometimes called me stubborn. They called me difficult. They didn't see a child scrambling for control in a world that was too loud, too overwhelming. I was trying to hold it all together, but they didn't understand the chaos inside me.

I learned to translate my pain into something quieter, something more acceptable. I became the good son. The one who didn't make waves. The smart one. The one who knew how to keep his head down and avoid trouble. But inside, there was always a storm.

There were four of us—siblings orbiting each other, always moving but never truly connecting. My brother was the golden child—polished, predictable. My sisters flickered between brilliance and burnout. And me?

I was the static. The outlier. The ghost in the room who

either talked too much or not enough, who laughed too loud or stood too still.

My youngest sister, Nina, though—she was different. She didn't flinch when I stuttered through stories or when I melted down halfway through a sentence. She never asked me to be smaller or quieter. She'd just sit next to me and wait, patiently, like my mess didn't bother her.

Her presence was permission.

Permission to be myself. Permission to be unpolished, unrefined, messy.

But the rest of the world wasn't built that way.

As I got older, the masking grew stronger. I learned how to make myself disappear. I turned my body into a weapon of politeness. Smiled on cue. Stood where I was supposed to stand. Played the part. Became the version of myself everyone wanted to see.

By high school, the gap between my inner self and the version I showed the world was vast. I had friends. I played soccer and tennis. I made jokes. I led small groups at church. But all the while, the dark passenger lived under my ribs, whispering the same rules of survival:

"Don't be too loud."

"Don't be too weird."

"Don't make them uncomfortable."

And I followed them like scripture.

In family photos, you'll see me smiling. But if you look closely, you'll see the tension in my jaw, the way my hands never fully relax. The eyes that never quite land on the lens, like I was trying to disappear, to become invisible while still being seen.

No one noticed. Or if they did, they called it maturity.

My parents meant well. They loved me the best way they knew how. But they didn't understand the language of my pain. And I didn't know how to translate.

So, I became fluent in silence.

Somewhere along the way, I started to believe that love

meant shrinking. That safety meant performance. That my worth was conditional. If I could just keep it together, maybe I wouldn't feel so broken. Maybe, I could be the person I thought everyone wanted me to be. Maybe I wouldn't feel like I was failing.

There's this photo of us—Christmas morning. I'm in flannel, holding a guitar, smiling like my teeth are made of glass. I remember that day.

I remember the silence after the presents were opened, the way I stared at the floor, wondering why I felt so empty when everything around me seemed full.

THE GHOST THAT CARRIED A NAME

I carry the weight of silence.
Not in words, but in breath.
In the places I didn't speak.
In the words I never said.
It sits in my bones,
Underneath my skin,
A name I never learned to wear.
The ghost that never left,
Always beside me,
Filling the spaces I didn't fill.

That's the thing about families shaped like fists. They don't always hit. Sometimes, they just close.

And if you're the soft one, you learn to brace. You learn to fold. You learn to disappear in a way that gets applauded. Because silence doesn't leave bruises. But it leaves marks. And I still feel them. Every time a friend, or someone I meet says, "You turned out fine."

I want to ask— Do ghosts ever turn out fine?

Because I became one. And no one noticed.

6

THE ECHO IN MY CHEST

The bell rang, but I didn't hear it until after my body had already flinched.

THE FIRST CRACK wasn't loud. Someone brushed past me in the hallway between classes. Just a shoulder. No apology. No second glance. But something inside me flinched so hard I forgot how to breathe.

Everything looked normal. Lockers opened and closed in metallic rhythms. Sneakers skidded, laughter broke like waves on linoleum. I walked through it, hood up, books in hand, another name on the attendance sheet.

But I wasn't there. Each breath felt stolen. The lights above flickered like warning signs. The buzzing wasn't sound anymore —it was sensation, crawling over my skin like static electricity building with no release.

I smiled when someone made eye contact. We locked eyes and nodded. We both said "Hey." My voice didn't tremble. My hands did.

The dark passenger whispered: *"You're good at this. Smile and no one will ask."*

By the time I sat down in history, I'd already left myself behind. My body moved through the motions: pen out, notebook open, nod at the teacher. But I was hovering just behind it, watching. Like the soul had slipped loose.

The boy behind me tapped his pencil once. Then again. And again. Each sound felt like it struck bone. There was a presentation later that afternoon. Group project. I'd rehearsed my part thirty times. I still couldn't remember the first line. I told myself I was just tired. That this was nothing. That if I made it to lunch, everything would reset.

The lie almost held.

In the locker room, boys shouted and laughed like they were made of noise. Someone flexed in the mirror. Another threw a sock. Shirts flew through the air like victory flags. I stayed dressed, fumbling through my gym bag like it had answers. My hands were damp. My armpits soaked.

I couldn't tell if I was hot or freezing. My heart was thudding against my ribs like it wanted out. A voice beside me. "Hey, you okay?" I nodded. "Yeah." Smiled. They moved on. I didn't.

By fourth period, the hallway had narrowed. The lockers leaned in. My vision turned watery around the edges. My ears popped. The air felt too thin. The floor tilted, just slightly. Like it didn't want to hold me.

Someone said my name. It sounded like it came through a wall. I walked like I was underwater. Don't stop. Don't run. Don't let it show.

I found the upstairs bathroom and slipped into the last stall, locked the door, and sat down with my backpack still on.

And I folded in. Hands over ears. Face buried in my jacket. No tears, just trembling. Like a pressure valve releasing steam before the machine exploded.

I tried to count.

Breathe.

Pretend.

Instead, memories surged.

I was five, under the table in Bolivia, rocking because the chairs were wrong. My dad's voice: "Get it together."

I was six, holding a pot in the living room, peeing into it without understanding why. My mother's coworkers staring like I was contagious.

I was twelve, blinking out during an assembly, a teacher asking if I was okay, and me nodding like my life depended on it.

Everyone in my orbit called me mature. Calm. Easy. I was drowning, silently. I didn't understand why.

A stall door slammed. Laughter. Footsteps. I didn't move. Furniture doesn't bleed.

The dark passenger hovered beside me. "*Let it pass. Don't break here.*"

When I finally stood, my legs wobbled. I found the mirror. The boy in the glass looked fine. Pale. Quiet. Nothing out of place. I smiled at him. Practiced. Perfect.

The dark passenger whispered again: "*You're almost invisible. Almost perfect.*"

Then I walked out.

English class came and went in vowels. Someone cracked a joke. I laughed with them. I couldn't tell what was funny.

At the end of class, I almost said it. To the teacher. Anyone. "I'm not okay."

The words came up. Hit my throat. Died.

I didn't say a word, but something shifted in the air.

Just as the words I couldn't say choked me, I felt something —the lightest touch, a hand on mine.

No words. No need to explain. Just warmth and presence. Julia. She was sitting across from me, her hand in mine, her touch grounding me in a way I hadn't felt in so long.

For that moment, everything stood still. The dark passenger disappeared into the background. Time seemed to freeze. The buzzing in my ears faded.

The world slowed down, the noise of the hallways, the

echoes of everyone's voices in my head. All of it paused. I blinked, not sure if it was real. But her hand was still there. Firm but gentle.

"You're okay," she said, her voice soft, steady. "Just breathe. I know what's going on. Shift your focus to the present."

And for the first time in a long time, I did. I focused on the feel of her hand, the quiet rhythm of her voice.

It wasn't magic. It wasn't a cure. But in that moment, Julia gave me a lifeline. She didn't fix me. She didn't ask questions. She didn't judge. She just saw me. The real me beneath the mask.

For a heartbeat, it was like surfacing from deep water. My lungs burned with air I hadn't realized I was holding. The noise didn't vanish—it dimmed, like someone had turned the dial down just enough for me to hear myself think. And in that space, small and flickering, a thought rose: *maybe I could speak. Maybe I could be heard.* It didn't last. But it was there. A splinter of possibility lodged under the skin.

At dinner, my mom asked how school was. "Fine," I said. I smiled. Took my plate to the sink. Said thank you.

Later, I stood in front of the mirror again. I tried saying something. Anything. "I'm still here." It sounded foreign. Like I'd stolen someone else's voice. I tried laughing. It echoed wrong. Like feedback from an empty speaker. The reflection stared back, unblinking. Rehearsed.

There was a sound in my chest. Not grief. Not even fear. An echo. The pressure of every unspoken scream vibrating through bone.

And beneath it, the dark passenger.

Calm.

Patient.

Finishing the smile I had started. *"Let them clap,"* he whispered. *"Let them love the echo."*

I opened my mouth. The static said, "Finally."

Tomorrow, the mask will crack in public. And no one will know what to do with what spills out.

THE HAND THAT STAYED

There was one time.
After another static storm.
I didn't sit alone.
A friend in English class touched my wrist without words.
No fixing. No questions.
Just weight and presence.
Her eyes didn't ask why. Her hand didn't flinch.
She didn't pull me back. She just didn't let me vanish.
Sometimes, that's enough to fracture the silence.
Sometimes, that's what keeps you tethered.

7

THE COST OF BECOMING

I wasn't destroyed in one blow. I was disassembled—ritually, obediently, with love.

I'M STANDING in line at Target with a red cart full of things I don't remember picking. She's behind me. Scrolling. One Air Pod in. The left one, always.

I speak. She doesn't.

The cashier says hi. I return the smile like a transaction. Too bright, too smooth. I'm good at this part. This mask. This language of being digestible. Every gesture a translation. Every breath, a lie shaped like a person.

The belt stutters forward. Almond milk. Oatmeal. Dog treats. Cough drops. Almond milk again.

She notices.

"I can't drink that," she murmurs, barely peeling her eyes from the screen. "It upsets my stomach."

I freeze. Milk in my hand like a confession. A crime I committed without meaning to. I want to say I'm sorry. I want to explain. But there's no time for nuance in public. Not when people are watching. Not when I'm already failing silently.

"We'll return it," I say, too soft.

She shrugs.

A gesture made of dismissal.

"Never mind. I'll drink it."

She says it like weather. Like the forecast had always predicted disappointment.

Like I should've dressed for it.

The cashier avoids my eyes. I reach for my wallet. My hands shake, and I don't know if it's the lights or the almond milk or the unbearable tightness in my chest. She pays before I can. No words. Just a swipe and silence.

Behind us, a jar falls. Glass explodes across the tile—loud, unapologetic. Everyone flinches.

I don't.

Because I was already broken.

She learned that tone from someone; I know the ghost it came from. But I don't say it. I never say it. There are things you swallow so long they become your blood. Because some truths carry teeth when spoken aloud.

THE FIRST WOUND
She said it like the weather.
Like she was reading off a forecast.
"You're exhausting."

I slip into the bathroom. Not because I need to pee. But because I need to disappear. The air smells like bleach and something pretending to be lemon. The kind of clean that feels like a warning.

No paper towels. Of course.

I wave my hand under the dryer. A scream erupts from the wall. Mechanical. Rabid. A frequency that punches through my skull and detonates behind my eyes.

Like an earthquake.

Like a tornado.

Like a siren.

I flinch. I always flinch. But I do it quiet. And for one breathless second, I envy the jar. At least it got to break out loud.

The dark passenger stirs in my ribs.

"They don't hear it like you do," it says.

"That's why they think you're the problem."

Its voice is older than mine. Older than language. It doesn't whisper anymore. It finishes my sentences. It speaks in the dialect of survival.

"You were never made for silence," it says.

"You were carved for echo."

I nod. Not to agree. Just to stay standing. Just to stay.

The louder the silence, the smaller I became. Until even my shadows apologized for being visible. It wasn't the arguments that splintered me. It was the way her voice never cracked.

The walls blurred. My body stayed. My mind didn't.

Vermont. 2011. A grad school cafeteria.

I had just returned from Bolivia after finishing my internship. As I stepped inside, I scanned the room like I always did—habit, maybe survival.

My eyes landed on a round table where two old friends were already sitting with someone I didn't recognize. I was relieved to see familiar faces. I grabbed my breakfast and made my way over.

I didn't acknowledge her.

I just started talking to my friends.

By the time I sat down, the table had filled. Familiar voices surrounded me, asking how the internship went, eager for stories. She stayed quiet.

Eventually someone said, "Oh Marianne, this is Chris."

"Oh, you're the famous Chris," she replied.

I don't know why, but I was cold. Guarded. "Yep," I said, and turned back to my friends.

After breakfast, I went to class. The only open seat was next to hers. Of course it was. We were paired for the first assignment.

She speaks French. Laughs at the same things. There's that third culture click—the moment you meet someone who understands what it means to belong nowhere.

"You're intense," she says. "But in a good way." I believed her. I don't know why, but I believed her.

She didn't flinch when I stimmed in study group. Just kept talking about the World Bank. She answered emails with paragraphs. We stayed up late comparing international development models and favorite foreign airports. I thought: maybe this is what recognition feels like.

We fell into rhythm. Nights laughing over coffee, hands brushing by accident and then not. She told me she loved my mind. I told myself it was enough.

THE GHOST OF YES
She said yes to the ring
Yes to the plane.
Yes to the plan.
But her voice never followed.
Just the echo of her mother's.

I proposed in D.C., in the gardens of the National Cathedral. The symmetry of it still guts me. A place built for worship. For vows. For echoes. Her hands were cold. Her yes was warm.

My master's program required a field-based thesis.

You couldn't just theorize, you had to build something that breathed.

My focus was Corporate Social Responsibility: how companies could justify community programs in financial terms, how impact could be measured, modeled, monetized—how doing good could still serve the bottom line.

I pitched the idea to a mining company operating in Fort Dauphin, Madagascar. The company was a multinational giant that practically owned the region, the roads, the port, the people.

They liked it. Offered me a full-time role. The job *was* the thesis. A case study wrapped in a paycheck.

But here's what I didn't say in the pitch, what I didn't yet understand the weight of. Her mother ran the program. Lilith. Director of Corporate Social Responsibility.

Which meant I wasn't just entering the company. I was walking into *her* house. And from the moment I accepted, every step I took was through a door she'd already opened.

I thought I'd earned it. In truth, I'd been drafted.

We moved to Madagascar. Mosquito nets. Shared reports. Purpose. She read aloud. I cooked. We pretended peace could be built from small domestic rituals. For a while, I believed we were becoming something.

One day we were sitting in Lilith's house, just across the street from ours. Her kingdom. Her rules. Her gaze felt like a test I hadn't studied for.

She looked at me and said, "I want access to your personal finances."

I blinked. "Why?"

"Because I want to know," she said. "I want to manage it."

I said no.

It came out quiet, but clear. Final. Or so I thought.

She said nothing at first. And Marianne? She said nothing.

Lilith told her to call off the engagement. She accused me of being ungrateful and secretive. That as my mother in law, she had every right to manage my personal finances.

Marianne didn't call off the engagement. But she didn't push back, either. Silence. A new language we both understood but didn't speak.

Over the years, Lilith slipped into the spaces between us. Into our money. Our housing. Our meals. "It's just practical," Marianne said. Practical like erosion. Like boiling.

I pushed back. I said we were adults. Professionals.

I said we needed a home that was *ours,* not curated by someone who still referred to her daughter "baby" and insisted on tracking our grocery list.

I tried to set boundaries. Simple ones. Just enough to breathe. Just enough to be.

But Marianne wouldn't have it. "I'm scared," she said.

"If we set boundaries, it will push her away. She'll think we're shutting her out completely."

And she did. Every boundary became an act of war. Lilith called me disrespectful. Told me I was the only one with a problem.

"I do this for all my daughters and their husbands," she said. "You're the only spouse trying to build walls."

But they weren't walls.

They were doors I was begging to close.

And Marianne would just sigh. That same sigh that felt like a sentence. "Why are you always making things harder?"

So, I stopped pushing.

I told myself it was compromise.

But it was surrender by another name.

THE MOTHER THAT NEVER LEFT

She wasn't in the room.
But her voice was.
Every argument had a ghostwriter.

In 2016, Marianne started a second master's degree in special education. We had moved back to the D.C area two years earlier. I was working with U.S. Government funded projects in the finance realm.

And just like that, I became her unofficial research subject.

She stopped loving me like a person.

Started assessing me like a pattern she'd been trained to recognize.

She took notes.

Labeled my pauses.

Counted my stumbles.

Eventually, she said I should get tested. That something was wrong. That I wasn't "processing" the world right.

I told her I was just tired. Stressed. That I was just overwhelmed. Just built differently.

But deep down, I knew what she saw. And I knew what it would cost me if I said it out loud. So I delayed it. For four years.

Four years of swallowing the question. Of dressing up confusion as control. Of calling survival a personality.

Then came the pandemic. The world slowed. But mine began to overheat.

It happened at a mall. Fluorescent lights stung like needles. Masked bodies moved in erratic rhythm. A toddler screamed— high, relentless, piercing.

Something cracked. In my chest. In my spine. In whatever part of me was still pretending.

My limbs turned to smoke. My hearing tunneled. My breath forgot its rhythm. I collapsed. Publicly. On a bench I couldn't rise from.

Vision white. Then flickering. Then gone.

No one stopped. No one saw a man vanish in plain sight.

No one noticed a body trying to remember itself.

That bench held more than my weight. It held the moment I stopped pretending.

I got tested. It was a process that involved lengthy questions about childhood, conversations with therapists. Just lots of questions.

After weeks of testing, in came the results.

THE FORGOTTEN PIECE

They named him broken.
Stamped it on his breath.
Tried to erase the shape of his storm.
But you can't amputate the truth.
You can only bury it.
And what we bury, learns how to rise.

Autistic. A diagnosis like a mirror that finally told the truth. I stared at it and saw myself. Not broken. Just wired in another language.

I told Marianne. She blinked slowly, like I'd spoken in static. She told Lilith.

The space between us bloomed. Wide. Silent. Unbridgeable.

Lilith smiled when she said it.

"You're defective."

"Marianne deserves normal."

"You're an embarrassment."

She said it like scripture. Like mercy. Like execution.

"Leave her. Or I'll make sure it happens."

Marianne said nothing to defend me.

"You're too much. You don't know how to function. You always make things harder." She said it softly. Like feedback. Like love recited as diagnosis.

At first, I fought it. I thought, I have a good job. I drive. I can function on my own. I wasn't like Rain Man. When I started telling people after the diagnosis, some said, "No, you're not autistic. You're normal."

That's how I knew the mask worked.

But after years of hearing that I was broken. Defective. That I should die, from both Lilith and Marianne, I stopped fighting. I started absorbing. I let the words settle into me like mold.

I stopped writing. I stopped singing. I stopped laughing in front of her.

I told myself it was maturity. Adaptation. Growth.

But inside I was folding. My body no longer a home, just a place to wait out the collapse.

THE CONDITION
I mistook disappearance for healing.
Silence for growth.
Compliance for love.

I nodded more. Spoke less. Curled in.

"Your autism is exhausting," she said one night, placing her fork on her napkin like punctuation.

After the diagnosis, comments like these became a constant refrain. Suddenly, I wasn't a man, I was a disorder with shoes on.

I thanked her. Smiled. Swallowed the shame like communion.

Later, brushing my teeth, I heard myself say it:

"God, I must be impossible to live with."

It wasn't her voice.

It was mine.

The dark passenger watched from the mirror.

"See?" it whispered. *"Now you're finally fluent."*

The body is a cathedral.

But mine was built for ruin. No choir, no sermon, no sanctuary. Just echo.

Sometimes I think I was holy once. Before the storm. Before the silence taught me reverence. Before the first time my mother pulled over the car, said nothing, and waited for the calm down from a mini autistic meltdown.

I learned then: my volume was dangerous. My presence, conditional.

The cost wasn't in what they said.

It was in what I stopped saying.

The cost wasn't in the scream.

It was in the stillness I mistook for peace.

The next morning, she asked what I wanted for breakfast.

I told her I wasn't hungry.

I didn't say I hadn't been in months.

THE MASK'S PRAYER

Let me be enough.
Let me be quiet.
Let me not need.
Let them not see.
Let them not leave.
Amen.

8

THE GIRL WHO SPOKE MY LANGUAGE

Some people don't save you. They remind you you're worth saving.

MADRID. 3 A.M. A cracked hostel window leaking moonlight. She's asleep beside me, one arm curled around a half-written page. Her breathing is slow, steady, like a secret being told again and again.

Outside, someone sings—soft, off-key, like they're mourning something not yet lost. I whisper the word she taught me that afternoon: *aşk*.

In Turkish, it means love. But not the kind you write in birthday cards. Not the kind that settles into comfort or safety.

No. *Aşk* is the kind that devours. It is the word for love when love becomes fire. When it does not ask permission. When it enters like a fever and leaves like a wound.

The Sufis use it to name the ache for God—that holy madness. The thirst that never sleeps. But it's also what you feel for the one who looks at you like a secret and suddenly your whole life becomes flammable.

Aşk is not "I love you." It's "I would shatter myself into light if it meant you could find your way home."

It is the kind of love that builds no shelter.

Only altars.

And then asks you to bleed on them.

It tastes like her name. It tastes like leaving. It sounds like something older than language—something ancient bleeding through the seams of the night.

There are moments you know, even as they're happening, will ruin you. This was one of them.

THE WORD THAT COULD NOT STAY

It sounded like her name.
It looked like a border I couldn't cross.
It felt like a hymn I wasn't holy enough to sing.
And somewhere beneath it, the dark passenger stirred—
hungry for a language it could not speak.

I still hear her voice when I get the Turkish word wrong—like a ghost tracing the edges of a memory I can't quite hold.

It doesn't sting.

It *reverberates*, like a string pulled too tight across the years. The kind of ache that asks, not why she left, but why I didn't follow.

Not in shame.

In rhythm. Like a second heartbeat. Like a name I forgot I had.

We met in the cafeteria at American University. I was halfway through a bland turkey sandwich when she walked past my table. She looked like someone who stepped out of a different century—like poetry wrapped in linen and dusk.

There was something otherworldly about her, the kind of presence that didn't just enter a room—it *shifted* it. She smelled like bergamot and sandalwood, like secrets passed through incense smoke.

She didn't walk.

She *glided*. As if gravity had made an exception—and I was the one still tethered to the floor. When she spoke, the cadence made you forget your own language, as if hers was the only one the body was meant to understand.

Her laugh floated across the room like it didn't belong to the air.

Her name was Asli. Turkish. Gorgeous. Her eyes laughed before her lips did. When she said my name for the first time, it felt rehearsed—like she'd known me in another life and had just been waiting for this scene to begin.

It wasn't dramatic. Just familiar. Like a phrase I should've already known the translation for. There was a slowness to her. Not lazy, not unsure—just deliberate.

She picked her words like fruit: ripe, necessary, fragrant with truth, and as carefully as someone lighting a candle in the dark— aware of the silence it might illuminate.

And when she spoke in Turkish, I didn't want subtitles. I wanted to become fluent. Not in the language. In *her*.

THE GIRL WHO SPOKE MY LANGUAGE

Some people are translation.
You don't notice them until the sound cuts out.
And then suddenly, nothing makes sense.
The dark passenger cannot translate love.
It only mimics silence.

I told her I wanted to learn.

She didn't offer flashcards. She offered *presence*.

Presence over coffee. Over laughter between classes. Over walks through the city. Over listening to Turkish music playing on her laptop.

As I learned her language, I can still see her handwriting looping across my notebook, teaching me not just vowels and consonants, but rhythm.

Istanbul stopped being a city and became a pulse I was chasing across every inch of her voice.

After she left American University the semester after we met —a departure that left me devastated—we continued dating long-distance.

Our Skype calls became lifelines. We were always planning the next time we'd see each other. And we did—during the summer after she left, we met up in Spain.

We started in Madrid and toured for days, wandering through museums, cafes, and crooked cobblestone streets. There was something deeply innocent about her. Protected, in a way. Like the world hadn't bruised her yet. She was dynamic in a quiet way, electric without noise.

We traveled by bus to Granada where we watched flamenco dancers stomp stories into the stage.

In Sevilla, we toured winding alleys and took a romantic horse-drawn carriage ride one evening. We saw Córdoba, wandered the Alhambra, and ended in Barcelona where we stood in front of Picasso and let color tell us what words couldn't.

We stayed in hostels, ate strange meals, and held hands across time zones. But even then, I knew the clock was ticking.

Every train ticket had a shadow.

Every night felt like the last one that wouldn't hurt. Time didn't pass with her—it perched. Performed tricks.

Vanished at the worst possible moment.

And still, it didn't stop there. I visited her in Turkey throughout my time at American. When she got accepted to a master's program in Hungary, I went there too. Later, when I began mine in Oman, I visited her again. We kept finding each other. Until, somehow, we didn't.

I was always watching her hands—how she spoke with them. How they moved when she told stories. Her hands were scripture in motion. They weren't just part of her—they were relics of the language we built between us. Her hands were the only prayer I ever whispered without guilt.

She spoke like someone who had long since made peace with silence. I hadn't. I filled it with noise. She let it breathe. Her stillness was its own gospel, and I was illiterate.

There were small ruptures I never named. The dark passenger watched them closely—measured each crack like it was counting down to collapse. Once, when I shut down mid-conversation and needed space, I panicked thinking I'd ruined everything. She simply handed me tea and said, "You don't have to disappear to breathe."

But I already had. The dark passenger had quietly taken my place, mimicking my smile, borrowing my silence. I was halfway gone and didn't know how to re-enter my body. I didn't know how to stay anywhere that didn't mistake silence for absence.

She saw me. Not the mask, not the mimicry. She saw beneath the passenger. Before diagnosis. Before the word "autism" gave me something to point to. Before I had language for why I flinched at fluorescent lights or couldn't stand certain textures. She didn't need the glossary. She translated me intuitively: the way I hesitated before hugging, the way I needed space without asking, the way I talked too much about the things I loved.

There was one night, over çay, when we talked about home.

She said hers was split between continents.

I said mine was drawn in airports. We both laughed, but hers was warm. Mine was hollow.

She didn't ask me to stay. But I wanted to. I wonder what would've happened if I had. But I wasn't built for staying—not yet. I was fluent in running, illiterate in permanence.

She once told me the Turkish word for love wasn't *Sevgi*, the polite kind. It was *aşk*.

"It means suffering that sings," she said, sipping her coffee. Like it was nothing. Like it was everything.

I didn't understand it then. I do now.

Because loving her wasn't about possession. It was about recognition.

And that kind of seeing? It scars.

Not violently.

But deeply.

The kind of scar that sings back.

We didn't end. We just faded—like ink on skin left out in the sun, like music you can hum but no longer sing.

The grief was quiet but stubborn, showing up in the spaces where her voice used to live.

No slammed doors. No betrayal. Just... distance. Geography. The timing that always seems to arrive with a smirk and a suitcase.

The last time I saw her, she waved from the other side of passport control. She smiled like she didn't know it would be the last time. I smiled like I did.

She left a version of me behind in Istanbul. A softer one. A boy who listened more than he explained. A boy who almost stayed. A boy who didn't yet know he would one day fall apart in an entirely different country, with no one to say his name the way she once did.

I don't remember the last thing she said to me. But I remember the silence that came after. The silence that learned my name. The silence that still speaks in her accent.

And sometimes, when I whisper her name into the dark, I hear it—just under my breath—*aşk*, sung in a voice I no longer know how to imitate.

And the worst part?

I'm not sure I want to forget it.

9

THE WAR AT THE EDGES

It didn't start with shouting. It started with silence. With smoke curling under the door, whispering that I was no longer welcome in my own life.

LILITH WASN'T STORM. She was smoke seeping into our walls, into Marianne's voice, into the space between sentences. By the time I realized I was choking, I was already used to the taste.

She didn't live with us. She lived between us. In the cushions. In the calendars. In the silences.

I remember Madagascar—Fort Dauphin, the wedding under the tree in her mother's yard in 2012. I was nervous, but the ocean held its breath for us. The silence then was sacred.

Not this. Not the kind of silence that comes from being drowned out. Not the kind that thickens between people like mold in the seams—quiet, fungal, inevitable.

Back then, it felt like we were choosing each other. Like even the wind leaned in to listen. Like her mother's yard bent toward blessing, and the tree under which we stood was witness, not weapon.

But over the years, that tree became a metaphor. She didn't just plant herself in our lives. She rooted, wrapped, consumed.

Sank into our money, our home, our hours, our words.

What began as ceremony decayed into control. The sacred turned surveillance. Stillness replaced by scrutiny.

And the ocean that held its breath for us? I think it's still holding it. Because what followed wasn't a marriage. It was a slow occupation.

After we moved back to Maryland in 2014, the distance made peace possible. But when she visited, the air turned sour. She dictated our schedules. Planned our trips. Scolded me like I was a child. Dismissed my background when it didn't fit her story. Like the time I told her I wasn't Bolivian. She called me a douchebag in front of her whole family.

And Marianne said nothing.

Even then, I tried. I kept saying we needed boundaries. But every time I brought it up, Marianne's eyes would flicker. "She's my only parent left," she'd say. "If I lose her, I lose everything."

So, I offered to speak. To be the messenger. To take the heat. But she told me not to. Said she'd handle it.

She didn't.

And Lilith 's voice became the only one in the house that mattered.

After I was diagnosed with autism in 2020, it got worse. The diagnosis brought me relief—it gave me language for what I had always been. But to Lilith, it was ammunition. "You're defective," she said in my own living room. "Marianne shouldn't be married to someone like you. It's bad for her mental health."

She said that Marianne should leave, and if I didn't make that happen, she would.

Marianne promised she'd talk to her. But nothing changed. That was the last time I believed the words without looking for the breath behind them.

THE CONDITION

They called it a diagnosis.
But it became a sentence.
I wasn't allowed anger. Or grief.
Or contradiction.
Because now I had a name.
And a name makes it easier to blame the body.

Marianne started saying things that weren't her words:

"You're exhausting."

"You can't function without me."

"I'm walking on eggshells."

The words moved through her like ventriloquism. Lilith had taken up residence inside her daughter's mouth.

There were documents on the kitchen table. "Items," as Lilith called them. "Just in case I ever need to leave you," Marianne said. Among the items were documents her mother had drafted, painting my autism as the source of Marianne's ruin—as if my very being had inflicted an irreparable wound on her mental health.

And with my diagnosis, the indictment deepened: suddenly she was not a wife, but a caregiver. A role she never chose, a role I never asked her to bear. We married without that word in the room, yet now it was being used as the excuse to unravel everything we had built.

I didn't argue. Arguing meant proving their point.

I stopped recognizing my reflection. It blinked like me—but it wasn't mine.

I began hiding things. Pay stubs. Poems. Any proof that I was still whole.

Marianne stopped asking me what I needed. She started asking Lilith what to do. Lilith began correcting our dogs. Our routines. Me.

Shadow started sleeping closer.

She was the only one who didn't flinch when I whispered, "I don't feel like myself anymore."

The mask wasn't slipping. It was crumbling in my sleep.

THE GODMOTHER OF CONTROL

She didn't need a key.
She entered through doubt.
She slept between our breathing.

The house began to turn. The window refused to open. The air grew heavier. Shadow barked at corners. I started sleeping with the closet light on—not for monsters. I already knew her name.

Lilith moved our wedding photo three inches to the left. I moved it back. The next morning, it was gone. Replaced by a picture of her and Marianne at the beach. I hadn't been invited to that trip. That was the point.

Marianne fell asleep with her phone still lit. Lilith 's name glowing like an ember on the pillow.

I stood in the hallway one night and thought: maybe I don't make it out of this.

I brushed my teeth.

I went to bed.

The silence stayed.

She already knew. That I tried to kill myself the year before in 2022. I drank antifreeze and survived by accident. She knew about the depression. The masking. The collapse.

She blinked.

Then asked me not to tell her mom.

Shadow lay by the door. Her ears twitching at sounds I no longer trusted. Guarding the last breath that remembered my name.

I passed the mirror on my way out. It didn't reflect me—just the ruins behind me, still trying to look whole.

The house didn't echo.
It exhaled.
And none of that breath was mine.

10

THE DREAM THAT CRACKED

Not all dreams shatter. Some just split slowly, under pressure.

WE BUILT a home on borrowed ground. With hands too tired to keep building.And hearts that cracked beneath the weight of pretending.

We thought we were planting roots. But the soil had already started to shift.

By the time we moved to Baltimore in 2016, we had already bounced through a string of temporary stops around Maryland and DC—Kensington, Bethesda, Fells Point, then Patterson Park. Each place a holding pattern. Each lease a quiet countdown.

In 2020, we finally said, "enough."

We wanted permanence. Or at least, the illusion of it.

I told Marianne I wanted something stable. A home. Somewhere that felt like *ours*. I didn't ask for much. A driveway. A newer build, something we wouldn't have to pour our savings into fixing up. A little space between us and the neighbors. I thought I had a voice in the search.

But slowly, that voice disappeared.

Marianne and Lilith took over. Lilith agreed to co-sign on the mortgage temporarily, and we made a plan to refinance her out of it. We did, a year later. The $10,000 down payment came from Marianne's inheritance—a gift Lilith reminded us of often. Every time I pushed back, she'd say, "That's my daughter's money," as if the act of giving had bought her permanent jurisdiction.

I remember walking out of a showing and saying, "I just want a driveway." Marianne didn't even look at me. Lilith said, "This isn't about your needs, it's about Marianne's stability." And just like that, I was no longer in the room. The house we bought wasn't new. It was a 1950s Cape Cod, crammed between other homes in a tight neighborhood in Riviera Beach, Maryland. No driveway. No buffer. And from the start, it needed work.

THE HOUSE THAT HEARD

We walked through it like it was already ours.
The floors creaked. The walls listened.
And something inside us whispered, this could be home.
But dreams echo differently in borrowed space.

I told myself it had good bones. That I could shape it into something I'd be proud of. We installed a driveway, redid the flower beds. I built a fire pit. Planted a dogwood and a Japanese maple. I had plans. We both did. New kitchen. Remodeled bathroom. Maybe one day, an addition.

But those plans kept getting buried beneath problems. A crack in the foundation meant the basement flooded when it rained. The air felt heavy with mildew and silence.

Every time I mentioned that we could have avoided this if we'd just chosen a different house, Lilith would snap: "I gave Marianne that inheritance. You should be grateful."

There was one room in the basement—unfinished, untouched. I'd meant to turn it into a man cave but never did.

The lightbulb dangled, always swinging. It felt like a confession waiting to be made.

THE ROOM THAT NEVER FORGOT
I was the room you avoided.
The space you promised to fill.
You left me hollow, but I remember.
I remember how you almost became someone else in here.

Tucked on a peninsula where the Stoney and Patapsco Rivers meet, Riviera Beach had its rhythm. Dogs barking. Old men sipping coffee. Lawn mowers before 9 a.m. In summer, it sang. In winter, it waited. And in the middle of it all, our house sat like a question we were too tired to answer.

Shadow and I had a walking route that hugged the water and led to a neighborhood park. Sometimes, that stretch felt like the only thing that still made sense.

Inside, things were different.

Marianne's job drained her. She was a Special Educator. As an Analyst for U.S. Government funded projects, mine did too.

But only one of us seemed to get permission to be tired. She told me I worked from home, so housework was *my* job. I cooked. Cleaned. Managed the bills. Tried to get us help. A financial advisor. A plan. But she didn't want to engage. Said money gave her anxiety. Said I was overreacting.

Every time I brought up boundaries, the cycle started again.

THE LINES THAT BROKE
I drew them in sand.
She washed them away.
Her mother rewrote them in stone.

Lilith visited more often since we bought the house. With each visit, the shaming grew sharper. At first, it was her—pulling

Marianne aside, whispering that I was too much. That my autism was a burden. That I'd never be stable.

When I told Marianne that really bothered me, she said, "I'll talk to her." But nothing changed.

Eventually, she joined in. Not all at once. Not loudly. Just small comments, like seeds dropped in passing.

"Maybe kayaking isn't safe for you."

"You get overstimulated when you run too far."

"You know the guitar's too loud when your nerves are like that."

"Chris, you're too sensitive."

"Chris, you can't handle the noise. You have sensory issues."

"Chris, stop playing guitar. It's too much for you."

Things I loved—things that made me feel like *me*—were slowly pulled from my hands, one justification at a time. And somewhere along the way, I stopped arguing. Because when they both said it, it started to sound like truth. I became the problem.

I stopped fighting. Let go of things I loved. Until she asked, "Why do you only rely on me? Why don't you have friends?"

But when I tried to go out, she'd ask, "Why are you being selfish? You can't handle that."

I started to disappear.

THE INVISIBLE MAN
I stood in the hallway.
I said I needed help.
They told me I was the hallway.

In March of 2023—almost three years after my diagnosis, nearly a decade into our marriage—when she asked for a divorce.

It came without warning.

Her grandfather had just died. We were sitting in the car, parked in silence, grief still clinging to the windows, when she turned to me like she was unburdening a secret.

"I was ignored by my mom," she said. "She gave all her love to my sisters. Because they have kids."

"We agreed we wouldn't have children," I said.

"I know. But your autism... it makes kids impossible. I want my mom's love. I need kids."

She said it like a confession. I heard it like a verdict.

"We agreed we wouldn't have children BEFORE we got married," I said. "That was before the diagnosis. Autism had nothing to do with that decision."

But part of me was already too tired to fight. Tired of being dissected. Tired of shrinking to fit her comfort.

Tired of being the problem in rooms where I was supposed to feel safe. So I said it: "Fine. You'll be better off with someone who can give you what you want." "I want you to be happy." I meant it. Even if it gutted me.

That shifted the conversation. Suddenly it wasn't about leaving anymore. "This was a bad idea," she said. "We need therapy." We tried.

The therapist named the abuse. Marianne flinched, then folded into denial. Counseling ended. And something between us—quiet, trembling, almost holy—shattered without sound.

When my mom visited in August of that year, she saw me— exhausted, empty, broken. Marianne was about to leave for Madagascar to visit Lilith My mom tried to help. Asked Marianne to support me more. Just a little. With the house. With the finances. With boundaries.

Days after her return, Marianne asked for divorce again. Said my mom had interfered. Said my autism was too much.

THE MASK THAT CRACKED
I tried to hold it together.
But my hands were full of apologies.
And the mask was heavier than my face.

She already knew about the suicide attempts. She knew how

close I'd come to ending it. I had told her. I had told my family. I was already in therapy. Trying.

After the second divorce call, I collapsed. I texted my sister: *I'm fading.*

Nina came to get me.

THE LIGHT THAT CAME
She didn't knock.
She didn't ask.
She just came.
And I let her in.

Marianne and I agreed to try one last time. A final gamble. Sell the house. Start over in Massachusetts. We found a buyer. I came back to help pack.

It took two weeks. We boxed up everything—our lives in one small PODS container.

I don't cry easily. The dark passenger doesn't allow it. But on the final night, standing in the empty living room, the weight of it crushed me.

It was dark. Quiet. The walls echoed. I looked around at what was left—the outline of a rug, the dust where our bookshelves used to be. And I broke.

I hugged Marianne. And I cried.

Not for her.

For the dream.

For the version of me that believed I could build a home in a house like that.

Before I walked out for the last time, I thought of Shadow. She had stayed behind with my sister. She didn't get to say goodbye to this place. I imagined her sniffing around the rooms, tail flicking, confused that the smells were fading, that the couches were gone, that the house no longer felt like home.

What would she have thought of this ending?

THE DREAM THAT CRACKED

It was never just about the walls.
It was about the voice I lost inside them.
And the boy who finally asked, "What about me?"

Sometimes, I still hear the sump pump in my dreams. The house sighing under the weight of rain it couldn't hold. As if it remembers I once called it home.

And as I locked the front door one last time, I caught my reflection in the glass.

I didn't recognize the man staring back. He looked relieved. Or maybe just empty.

I didn't wave. Neither did he.

Let him stay there.

Let him haunt it, if he needs to.

I was already walking away.

And this time, I didn't look back.

Part Two

MEMORY AND ROOTS

Before we named the wound, we called it family.
We wore their silence like skin.
What we inherited wasn't love. It was survival dressed in tradition.
Memory doesn't knock. It breaks in.
Roots don't ask if the soil was toxic.

11

THE YEAR I LEARNED TO STAY

She didn't rebuild me. She held the mirror still while I figured out how to stop disappearing.

BEFORE I KNEW how to stay, I mastered the art of vanishing. Not dramatically. Not with slammed doors or packed bags. But quietly. Invisibly.

In soft, practiced increments.

Skipping class. Missing meals. Smiling just enough to keep suspicion at bay. Fading into bookstores where silence looked like self-care.

I wasn't lost. I was erasing myself. Piece by piece.

It was late 2004. I came back home to Massachusetts. But I hadn't returned to anything whole. Massachusetts was just where the wreckage washed up. Trinity had collapsed under my feet— its rules, its rituals, the quiet shame I carried like scripture. I left without warning, without ceremony, without a plan. One minute I was walking across campus. The next, I was back in my home state, standing in a kitchen that hadn't changed, holding a body that no longer fit.

I still remember that last chapel service. The way the lights hummed too loud overhead. The smell of coffee and cheap cologne bleeding into the carpet. A professor whispered something about grace while the girl beside me prayed through tears. But I couldn't feel anything—not even God. Just a kind of hollow static. Like I'd been fasting from myself for too long and forgot how to return.

I stood up halfway through the final hymn. Walked out the back. Never went back.

My parents were overseas. In 2003, my mom accepted a role for a non-profit in Bolivia, and they left. We still kept the house in Ashland, but rented it out.

The house felt like a memory I didn't belong to. I slept late. Read books I didn't finish. Enrolled in night classes I never told anyone about. I wandered the aisles of Borders like a ghost who couldn't decide what kind of life to haunt.

My mother watched the drift from a distance. When she called, she'd ask how classes were going. I lied. She asked how I was feeling. I deflected. Eventually, she named it: ADHD. Maybe she was right. Or maybe she just needed something to blame. Something that sounded clinical. Containable.

But the truth was quieter than that.

I was lost. I didn't know what I was looking for. But I knew I was breaking.

And then, one day—soft as breath—she said it. "Have you ever heard of Landmark College?"

She'd heard it on NPR. A school for students like me. Neurodivergent. Unfinished. On fire beneath the surface. She was coming home on leave and said we could tour it together. "I think they might get you," she said. "The way you learn. The way you think. Maybe they can give you some structure."

She didn't say it as a fix. She said it like a door. Like she knew I was standing in the ruins of something I couldn't name.

I nodded. Not because I was convinced. But because something inside me—something bruised and half-asleep—leaned toward it.

Sometimes it only takes one person to believe you're still salvageable.

And that was the beginning.

THE BOY WHO COULDN'T STAY

He could cross oceans. Learn languages. Adapt to any current. But staying? That was different.
He mistook stillness for stagnation.
Mistook discomfort for doom.
Mistook help for judgment.
He ran before the room could empty.
Before the silence could accuse.
Before anyone could ask why he flinched when they said "normal."
He didn't mean to leave.
He just didn't know how to stay.

The hills didn't feel holy. Not at first. Just another detour. Another maybe. Another "what if this doesn't fix me?"

It was a two-hour drive from Ashland, up through the backroads of Massachusetts and over the Vermont border. Past dying leaves and winding rivers. Into a town so quiet it felt like it had made peace with itself. Putney. Small, still, surrounded by the White Mountains like cupped hands.

Landmark was quaint. Almost shy. But the way they spoke about structure lit something in me I hadn't felt in years. They weren't offering discipline—they were offering design. A chance to understand how my brain worked, not fix it. A chance to ask for what I needed without shame.

Self-advocacy. Executive function. Sensory integration.

Words I hadn't known I needed.

And for the first time, someone said, "You're not broken. You just learn differently." For the first time, I didn't feel like an accident. I felt... seen.

Maybe this was the place. Maybe here I could finally learn why I had always felt like a guest in my own skin.

And so, I applied. And I got in.

But I wasn't ready.

My family was still in Bolivia. I begged them to return. And they did. They listened and came back. Back to my childhood home in Ashland. Back to my side.

But I was still masking—flashing teeth I didn't feel, laughing like I had a pulse. Still spinning plates I'd already dropped, hoping no one noticed the crash had already happened.

The dark passenger thrived on the illusion.

I became magnetic. Flung charm like confetti and prayed no one looked too close.

He whispered in my ear during every late-night hangout:

"Keep them laughing. Keep them close. Keep yourself hidden."

I wasn't doing the work. Not any of it.

My parents visited. They met with Carol, my academic advisor. I wasn't invited. I didn't need to be. I knew what she would say.

Carol didn't lie. She told them everything: My academic probation. My disappearing act. The paper-thin mask I'd wrapped around my failings.

At lunch, they didn't yell. They didn't flinch. They gave me two choices: Come home. Or fund it myself.

I looked down at the plate in front of me. I still remember the way the fork caught the light—how the tines shimmered like teeth. I wanted to scream. I wanted to vanish. But all I could do was grip the edge of the table and say, "Fine."

If I was going to self-destruct, it wouldn't be on their dollar.

I finished what was left of the semester and left. Packed my Mitsubishi Eclipse. Drove toward the edge of the map.

Toward Tracie.

I met her in a fan chatroom for a book called *A Million Little Pieces*. Somewhere in the static of the Landmark blur. What started as casual posts turned into private messages. Then phone calls. Long conversations that stretched deep into the night. Late-night obsessions and long-distance laughter. Something strange and steady. During my semester at Landmark, I even went to visit her during Winter Break.

We became close. I enjoyed her. She was fifteen years older than me—I was twenty-one at the time. She was funny, sharp, and unflinchingly direct. She had a strong personality, knew what she wanted, and made no room for bullshit.

She lived alone, in her own place in Jacksonville, Florida. She worked for a major insurance company as a Compensation and Benefits Analyst. Solid. Self-sufficient. Rooted. A contrast to everything I was still fumbling toward.

When I showed up at her door, she didn't ask why.

She just opened it.

I took a job at Circuit City.

Clocked in. Zoned out. Lost in the fluorescent haze.

Days bled into each other like fog. I began to forget what I used to want. That was the danger—not despair, but drift. A quiet drowning. I was still learning how to stay.

Her friends became my circle. Older. Warmer. Unbothered by the way I hovered like someone still half-unpacked.

But Tracie saw me. Not the mask. The restlessness underneath.

She taught me how to live in a house without apology.

To cook.

To clean.

To breathe.

She domesticated me, yes—but more than that, she built a soft place in the world where I could put my name.

There was a chipped blue mug she used every morning.

It became my lighthouse.

One night, I came home from a long shift at Circuit City. My feet ached. My soul felt thin.

Tracie was waiting for me at the kitchen table, arms crossed, eyes flaring with something between worry and disappointment.

It was frustration wrapped in love.

"You're marriage material," she said, shaking her head,

"but not like this. You've got fire, but you're pretending to be a spark."

She paused, then said it slowly, clearly: "You work retail like your life depends on it—but you're burning out for something that doesn't feed you. Get it together. Live like you want to be chosen. Go back to school."

And somewhere in my chest, a match caught flame. It became my second lighthouse.

A few days later, a man walked into Circuit City.

Talked to me like I was made of static.

Asked for "bluetooof" computers.

Mocked me.

Undermined me.

And I snapped.

Not outwardly. Inward.

I saw the mirror. I saw what she saw.

THE WOMAN WHO HELD THE FRAME

She didn't rebuild me.
She didn't reach for the broken edges.
She just stood there—mirror in hand,
while I relearned the shape of my face.

The first time I felt still was in her kitchen. Tracie had just made chili.

The scent of onion and cumin clung to the air like something sacred.

There was music playing—Fleetwood Mac, maybe. I don't remember the song. I remember the silence between verses.

I remember my hand around the warm bowl, and how it didn't shake. She didn't glow.

She didn't preach.

She just remained—like a lighthouse refusing to apologize to the storm.

Her house smelled like hope had once lived there and decided to stay.

The chipped mug. The slow hum of her breath as she moved through her rituals. She gave me a room. A routine. A reason to wake up.

One night, she told me about the first apartment she ever lived in alone.

"I slept with the lights on for a year," she said.

"I was scared of the silence, until I learned it was mine."

And maybe that's why she understood.

She didn't ask me for anything but presence. She didn't try to fix me. She just let the storm settle in a quiet place.

There was one night I packed my bag. I don't even remember why. I just felt the weight of being seen and mistook it for danger.

She found me in the driveway, keys in hand. She didn't ask me to stay. She just said, "Take your time," and went back inside. I stood there in the dark for an hour. Then unpacked.

I vacuumed like I was cleaning up a crime scene no one noticed. Cooked like survival was a recipe. Laughed like I didn't hear the ticking. I began to breathe without earning it.

The dark passenger came with me. He lingered at the threshold like he wasn't welcome. He didn't pace. Didn't whisper. He just watched. Like a shadow learning stillness for the first time.

But sometimes, I could feel him behind me—teeth bared in silence, waiting for me to flinch.

There was one night we danced. No reason. Just music and light. It wasn't romantic. It was something better. It was presence without pressure. It was her saying, "I'm not asking you to heal. I'm just glad you're here."

I'd wake up and make eggs. She'd pour coffee. We didn't speak every morning. Sometimes the silence was the point.

Sometimes the silence held its breath, waiting to see if I'd vanish again.

Before I arrived at Tracie's, I'd once gone three days without speaking to anyone.

Missed a final.

Didn't even email the professor. I walked the campus at 3 a.m. and imagined dissolving. Not dying—just ceasing.

Becoming absence. I thought that would be mercy.

But in Tracie's house: I made pancakes. And for the first time, something whispered *"You can begin again."* I folded laundry.

I started writing again.

I filled a journal and didn't tear out a single page. I didn't know what any of it meant. But it meant I was still here.

THE CHIPPED MUG

It wasn't the mug she gave me.
It was what it carried. Warmth I didn't deserve.
A shape I didn't shatter.
The first object I held without breaking.

A few days after the Bluetooth incident, Tracie said the thing I couldn't unhear: "You're not living to your potential."

She didn't yell. She didn't plead. She just said it—flat, steady, with the kind of silence that dares you to disagree.

And I broke. Not loudly. Not all at once. But something inside me cracked—finally—beneath the weight of all the half-lived chapters I'd kept trying to outrun.

Because she was right. I hated that she was right. Hated that I had nothing to offer back but silence. But mostly, I hated the version of myself that was okay being left behind.

I'd spent my whole life sprinting toward fresh starts, only to bail before anything could root. College. Friendships. Identity. Half-built temples. Half-written names. Always running. Always disappearing.

And now my peers were graduating. Launching into careers. Rising.

And I was standing still. Fading. Watching the life I could have had drift out of reach—again.

I once skipped class for a week straight and sat in my car outside campus, pretending I wasn't coming undone. No one noticed.

So, I stopped lying to myself and I made a plan. Not for redemption, not for applause. Just to finish something I started.

I wrote to my academic dean and advisor. Not with excuses, but with a vow. Let me back in. One semester. No safety net. Let me show you who I am now. I knew full well my GPA had cratered to 1.6, below Landmark's academic standard.

But I ran the math. If I got straight A's this semester, I'd be halfway through Landmark's program with a GPA I could survive. If I kept going, I could finish with a 3.4. Enough to transfer to a reputable traditional academic institution. Enough to stop bleeding.

I hit send and held my breath. A few days passed and silence. Then one morning, a reply. They said yes. Landmark let me back in, but on probation. One semester. No second chances.

I had two weeks to prepare. I quit my job at Circuit City. Spent the rest of the summer with Tracie—her porch, her quiet faith, her calm that never asked for proof.

She didn't tell me I could do it. She just looked at me like I already had.

The day before I left, I called my mom. "Can I stop at the house?" I asked. "Just to rest before I drive back to Landmark."

There was silence. Then: "Wait... what?"

I told her everything. That I'd convinced them to let me back in. That I'd been accepted. That I was going back.

She didn't know what to say. Then she said yes.

I didn't realize until that moment how much I needed her to.

THE VOW UNDER ASH

Not all vows are spoken. Some are built in bone.
Forged in the ruins we ran from.
Signed in the breath we nearly gave up.
This one was carved quietly—
beneath porch light.
under the weight of a gaze that didn't flinch.
within a silence that didn't demand redemption.
No choir. No altar.
Just a backpack zipped like armor. A list scribbled on a gas receipt.
A whisper only the dark passenger heard.
The vow wasn't loud. But it burned.
And where there was once smoke,
he chose to kneel.
To stay. To rise.

So I drove north. Back to Landmark. Not as the boy who left, but the one who chose to return.

She hugged me before I left. Said she was proud. Told me to call if I got in trouble. Or if I had a terrible dad joke.

This time, I took the scripture seriously. Class schedules. Color-coded planners. Accommodations filed in triplicate.

Structure wasn't a cage. It was a sacred system. A cathedral for the divergent. A blueprint for breath.

But the dark passenger didn't stay quietly. That final week before I left Tracie's, he started coming back slowly.

His voice seeped through the cracks like smoke under a door. *"You think grades will make you worthy?"*

"You'll fail again."

"You always do."

But this time, his voice cracked. Just a hairline fracture. Just enough to let light through. Because I didn't run. I stood still. And I rose.

I got straight A's that semester. And the next. And the next.

Every one a blade in the ribs of the voice that told me I couldn't.

Every one a quiet scream: I'm still here.

I graduated with my Associates. My grades were good enough to transfer to American University in Washington, DC.

Landmark wasn't a detour. It was the furnace. The sacred fire where the broken were reforged.

A place where structure became scripture. Where self-advocacy became sacrament.

Where I learned to name myself before the world could do it for me.

I still use what they taught me. Not just to study. To live.

And I couldn't have done it without her.

Tracie. Her porch light. Her silence that held me. Her presence that never once asked me to be anything but becoming.

Tracie came to my Landmark graduation and sat in the crowd, smiling. It meant the world to me.

But there's something I regret.

I gave a speech when I received my diploma. I thanked everyone—faculty, staff, my parents. Everyone but her.

It wasn't on purpose. I was nervous, caught in the swirl of emotion. And I forgot the most important name.

I forgot to thank the person who helped me remember how to stay. That omission still lingers in my chest like a name half-said in a dream.

When I graduated from American University, I mailed her a photo in my cap and gown. Years later, I sent her a picture of the ocean. No caption. Just the horizon. Maybe it was my way of saying: I'm still learning how to stay. But look—I'm still here.

She responded with a heart emoji. That was enough.

We didn't last forever. She wasn't supposed to.

Tracie was a season. A sanctuary. A chapter that reminded me I didn't need to be fixed. I just needed somewhere to land.

THE ROOM I DIDN'T FLEE

No doors slammed.
No voices raised.
Just silence. And this time, I didn't run from it.

She never said goodbye like it was a wound. And when I left her house, I didn't feel like a ghost.

I felt like a boy who had stayed long enough to begin again.

And this time, I didn't run. I stayed. I rose.

The silence didn't swallow me—it crowned me.

And the dark passenger's voice finally whispered:

"You can begin again."

But this time, it sounded like her voice.

12

THE BORROWED NORMAL

Some places hold you like memory. Others like myth. But a rare few hold you like you were never broken at all.

LANSING, Illinois didn't greet me with arms. *She* did.

My grandmother conjured the whole town—through her porch light, her Sunday sauce, her voice echoing down the block like gospel wrapped in gravel.

My life was always changing. Bolivia. Thailand. France. New house. New language. New rules. But Lansing stayed the same. Her house was a frozen frame of constancy, a sacred holdout against the erosion of time. My earliest memories of going there start around age six. She would cart me around to grocery stores, malls, and let me be a normal kid. We'd go to summer carnivals, or take quiet walks in the forest preserves near her home. She always made time.

She didn't just give me normal. She let me borrow hers.

A few weeks each summer, Lansing opened its cracked sidewalks and let me slip between dimensions—into a town stitched from baseball games, charcoal smoke, and the hum of something I didn't yet have words for: belonging.

Even in the basement, the light felt different every summer I'd come visit. Like it was searching for something it didn't want to lose. Like it had started grieving before the rest of us.

It was the '90s. Bikes were our thrones. River Oaks Mall was our palace. My cousins and I skated at roller rinks, chased fire-flies on front lawns, prank-called Jenny Craig on pay phones with sticky fingers and Kool-Aid breath.

Kids still rode in the backs of pickup trucks. No FaceTime, no cell phones. Just laughter echoing down cracked sidewalks and the smell of grilled hot dogs thick in the air.

My grandmother's house was the heart of it all.

A tiny house on a quiet block—one and a half baths, three bedrooms, a half-finished basement, and a kitchen that smelled like garlic, Aqua Net, and history.

She was the kind of loud that made people sit up straighter. Italian-American, a waitress most of her life, never wealthy, never weak. She wore her opinions like perfume and made pasta by hand.

She had a saying for everything:

"If the sauce sticks to the spoon, it's done."

"Don't trust anyone who doesn't salt their pasta water."

"If you're going to cry, do it with your shoulders back."

Her voice was gravel and warmth. Her hugs lingered. Her house didn't just smell like dinner—it smelled like permission.

Even the dark passenger—the one who gnawed at my insides, who whispered that I was broken—stayed silent in her house. He didn't like The Price is Right, but he'd hush when she watched it. He paced outside her kitchen like a wolf in a cathe-dral. Her cooking turned his hunger into silence.

Sometimes I'd sleep in the semi-finished basement with my cousins. The room had wood-paneled walls frozen in the '60s, a bar with stools that spun, a pool table we weren't allowed to lean on, and a red rug that looked like it bled when the light hit it right.

My uncle slept in there usually like he was behind a curtain. There was a locked cabinet we weren't allowed to touch. I always thought it held tools. Sometimes I imagined it held ghosts.

It wasn't a basement. It was a chapel of the half-formed. Half-finished walls. Half-grown boys. Half-spoken prayers. We descended into it like pilgrims, surrounded by wood paneling that smelled like 1963 and ghosts that hadn't yet learned how to haunt properly.

That basement didn't hold furniture. It held proof—that I had once been safe.

I never met Max, her old German Shepherd, but some dogs don't die. They become part of the house. I'd feel him in the air —one breath warmer than the others. The floorboards would groan like they remembered his weight. Like they still needed him.

She always called at least once a week. Even when I was a kid, scattered across time zones and continents, she made sure I knew I hadn't drifted too far. Wherever I was in the world— Bolivia, Ghana, Ecuador—she sent care packages. Just because.

Always the same kind of thing. VHS tapes. Tang. Candy she probably shouldn't have mailed. Little slices of America that smelled like her house. The boxes were padded with grocery flyers and folded napkins. Like she wanted even the packing to feel familiar.

I didn't know what it was called then. But she lent it to me anyway.

When I started college in Illinois, she would come visit me, take me out to lunch, or invite me to her house. She always asked about school. Always listened.

She spoke to me the longest when she'd call. Asked the right questions. She didn't understand why we moved overseas, but she never judged.

"Why can't you just stay?" she would ask. "Why do you hate America?"

She didn't say it with malice. Just grief. Just longing. Just love.

She once told me, "You're always somewhere else, even when you're here." I didn't understand it then. Now I know—she saw the mask before I did.

There was something about that last summer—like the light was trying to memorize her face. Like time itself was holding its breath.

Years later, I was in Madagascar when I got the call.

Cancer.

I flew to Illinois to be with her. Stayed with her for two weeks when she got out of the hospital. She was laughing again. Eating again. The pasta was back on the stove. I thought maybe we beat it.

So, I flew back to Madagascar.

THE LAST MEAL I DIDN'T FINISH

She made pasta.
I saved the rest.
But I never came back.

Not long after I got back, she went back in. ICU. Her body fading into angles. My mom sent me a photo and said she looked like that painting—*The Scream*. And she did.

"She's refusing to die," my mom said over the phone.

"Why?" I asked.

"She wants to see you have kids."

"Put me on speaker," I said.

My voice cracked: "Grandma, it's okay to go when you're ready. I'm not going to have kids. I love you. I love you so much."

She couldn't speak. But she heard me.

And then the line went quiet.

The dark passenger didn't speak that day. He just stood

behind me, smiling. He knew what it meant to lose the only person who ever scared him.

THE DAY THE AIR WENT SILENT

The phone clicked.
The world stilled.
And somewhere, pasta cooled on a stove
that would never boil again.

Sometimes I still feel her in the breeze. In the scent of oregano. In the static before a VHS tape starts. In the hush that follows the first snowfall.

In the cold plastic of a phone receiver. In the softness of old grocery flyers.

Lansing is different now.

The mall is dying. The roller rinks are gone. My cousins have kids of their own. But that house still holds something sacred. A presence. A permission. A relic.

Lansing doesn't remember me. But sometimes, I think it remembers her. A flicker in the curtains. A light in the kitchen when no one's home.

Sometimes I think she visits in the scent of garlic and old TV static. Just long enough to remind me: I was once held without condition.

THE NAME SHE GAVE ME

Not a nickname.
Not a word.
Just belief, worn like a coat I didn't know how to carry.

I don't know what kept her in Lansing. Maybe it was comfort. Maybe it was nostalgia. We asked her to move in with us when we settled in Massachusetts. Every time she visited, she seemed so happy. So at peace.

I remember one summer evening in Falmouth, Massachusetts—we were sitting on the beach. She was in a beach chair, hand raised to the wind. Just waving. Like she was saying goodbye to something only she could see.

She didn't just give me normal. She built it into me—brick by brick, garlic by garlic, VHS by VHS.

And I carry it—like a relic. Like a name. Like a spell passed down in sauce-stained aprons and ghost light.

And wherever I go, I set the table for her.

A plate. A story. A silence thick with garlic and grace.

Because maybe—if the wind is just right—she'll sit down again.

Not just to eat. But to bless the boy I was, the man I'm becoming, and the ghost she never stopped guarding.

THE BLESSING

She didn't give me answers.
She gave me a chair at the table and said:
Eat.
Breathe.
Come back when you need to.

13

THE DIRT THAT DARED ME TO RISE

Some places break you. Some try to erase you. But a few rare places
—if you let them—teach you how to rise.

THE FIRST TIME I returned to the Grace Trail in Plymouth, I wasn't walking—I was searching. For breath. For stillness. For a reason to stay alive in a place that had forgotten me, or maybe that I had forgotten first.

Shadow trotted beside me, quiet and watchful. Spring pressed its green fingertips into the soil, trying to open the world again. The frost was still receding. My breath still shallow. But the trail—this trail—somehow remembered me.

I walked it like a man retracing a spell, one syllable at a time. Not just with my feet, but with my breath. Trying to see if the land still knew my name. Trying to believe I could come back to life here. The osprey returned before I did. Everything I buried in this place kept growing without me.

This wasn't just a trail. It was a witness. A mouth. A cathedral built from wind and ash. It didn't just wait—it summoned. It didn't whisper—it branded.

There are markers along the path, one for each letter in GRACE: Gratitude, Release, Acceptance, Challenge, Embrace. GRACE didn't ask. It beckoned. Each letter wasn't a prompt—it was a door. And I had to bleed to pass through it.

Each letter became a threshold. A breath I hadn't earned yet. A promise I didn't know how to make.

One morning, my sister and I walked the trail together, just after the osprey returned. She pointed out the ice thinning over the marsh. I didn't say much. She didn't ask me to. We just walked. The silence between us did the holding.

I remember catching fireflies behind the old Ashland house. My sister's laughter somewhere in the distance. The sky that night looked like it forgave me. I didn't know it yet, but I belonged here long before I returned.

THE ROOT THAT BLED

Gratitude is a bruise you touch on purpose.
Not to suffer—
but to remember it didn't break you.

We passed by the first GRACE Trail marker. Gratitude asked: *What am I grateful for?* I was grateful for her quiet. For the way she let me grieve in motion.

For winding roads, cranberry bogs, and historic ruins that outlast the people who built them. For marshes that listen better than most people I know.

For the osprey who watched me without flinching. For the daffodils that bloomed, for leaving, for masking, for surviving when I didn't want to. And still, they bloomed.

Earlier in 2025, when spring finally broke the frost, Ava and I walked the trail with Shadow. At the turn where the field opens to the ocean, I kept on the path while they veered right—Ava's hair catching the wind, Shadow racing beside her. For a moment, they looked like peace itself, as if the trail had been waiting for them too. I felt the weight of it—how lucky I was to have her, how undeserving I still believed myself to be, and yet how gently she stayed. Shadow followed her like a traitor, as if loyalty had shifted overnight. Even now, when I walk alone, she still pulls toward that turn. Part of me wonders if she's still hoping to find Ava there.

Even then, I could feel him at the edge of the field, waiting. The dark passenger never liked gratitude. It made him flicker.

As I continued to walk the trail, one day it hit me. Twelve years had passed since I left Massachusetts for Madagascar. And now, after the ward, after the unraveling, I was finally back.

When I first moved here in 1997 as a kid cracked open by culture shock, I didn't think I'd ever come to love this place — not the cold, not the silence that meant something different here, not the way the air bit back and expected you to keep walking. But somehow, over time, this land carved itself into me.

I never stopped needing the state I'd always call home. And when the sky caved in and I had nowhere left to go, Massachusetts didn't throw me a rope—it gave me ground.

It didn't heal me. It dared me to live again. I wasn't grateful because it was easy. I was grateful because it didn't kill me. I was grateful because I stayed.

The trail remembered.

THE LUGGAGE OF GHOSTS
Some bags are packed in silence.
Some are emptied by fire.
Some ghosts only leave when you do.

Release asked: *What do I need to release?* The past. The myth of constant movement. The ache I carried like proof. The performance. The polish. The passport full of masks.

I wasn't just fluent in languages—I was fluent in disappearing.

Every new country became a costume change. Every job, a script.

Charm was my currency. Silence, my sanctuary. I called it freedom. It was exile. Motion was the myth I sold myself to avoid being seen.

I wore normal like armor. Pressed. Smiling. Breathless. But the trail didn't want the version I'd rehearsed. It wanted the one I buried.

Release didn't whisper. It carved. It ripped the name tags off every version of me I'd performed just to survive. It made me watch them burn.

No more new airports. No more elegant escape routes.

This time, I'd have to stay. This time, I'd have to let the ache breathe. This time, I'd have set the mask on fire.

Release demanded I surrender the weight I had mistaken for identity. It came slower. More violent. It scraped its name into my chest. I've said too many goodbyes in too many airports. Flight routes drawn like borders. Me—a citizen of the in-between. I let go of Bolivia. I let go of exile. I let go of the mask. I let go of the narrative that said I had to prove my worth by running.

This wasn't nostalgia. It was an exorcism. The trail did not flinch.

THE MIRROR IN THE WIND

What if you are not broken?
What if the crack is the map?
What if the wind was never trying to undo you—
but to reveal you?

Acceptance asked: *What do I need to accept?* That I am different. That I am rebuilding. That the mask was never armor—only delay. In the CVS parking lot off 3A, I sat in my car with the door open, counting the seconds between sobs. The air smelled like crushed pine needles and asphalt. No one noticed. No one needed to. The wind stayed.

Massachusetts doesn't ask for perfection. It asks for presence. I've broken in stairwells, in pharmacies, in empty parking lots under a November moon. This place doesn't require me to explain. It listens in stillness. The dark passenger watched from the passenger seat as I wept. Said nothing. Just waited to be let in again.

I am autistic. I am root-bound. Acceptance didn't arrive like a sunrise. It arrived like a bruise that stopped hurting when I stopped hiding. The trail saw my mask fall. It did not look away.

THE EDGE OF RETURNING

When the car growled, I flinched.
When the wind screamed, I stayed.
Sometimes survival means not leaving.
Sometimes it means not finishing the drive.

Challenge asked: *What is my next challenge?* To stay. To choose not to escape, even when escape feels easier.

When I returned to the trail, it was after the ward. After everything cracked. I had sold my first home. The person who vowed to love me in sickness and in health tried to erase me instead—and now she was gone.

All that remained was aftermath. A silence with teeth. An apartment that tasted like panic. I couldn't breathe in those walls anymore. Every time I tried, I saw her—eyes sharp, voice seething. The knife in my hand. Her words like poison: *Do it. Kill yourself.*

I wanted easy for once. But rebuilding is never easy.

It's slow.

It's sacred.

It's staying when every bone screams *run.*

I imagined packing a bag and vanishing. I didn't have to imagine hard. The bag was already half-packed. And one day, I walked to the car like a man trying to escape his own body.

The engine turned over with a growl that sounded like good-bye. But the road held still. It stared back.

It didn't whisper. It bared its teeth. And something in me flinched. I wanted the exit. But the wind said: *Not yet.* The trail said: *Finish this.*

My state is not soft. It does not coddle. It holds you down and dares you to rise. Some days I cursed it. Some days I thanked it. Most days I did both. The dark passenger still walks behind me now—but further back. As if the salt in the wind burns his name from the air. He stirred once. But the trail would not let him pass. Even he was afraid of the daffodils.

Challenge wasn't a battle. It was a contract.

THE PLACE THAT DARES

Not every war is loud.
Some ask you to stay.
Some dig their claws in so you remember you belong.
This land doesn't free you—it remakes you.

Embrace asked: *What can I embrace as possible?* The soft return. The unspectacular miracle of staying. Of roots. Of breath. Of silence that doesn't punish.

On a separate occasion, I returned to the trail with Shadow. She chased something I couldn't see and barked at the wind. I laughed—really laughed—for the first time in weeks. The trail didn't change. I did.

The hardest part of healing wasn't surviving. It was letting myself hope again.

For a long time I mistook hope for a trick. A mirage built to lure me back into the fire. But on that trail, with salt air in my lungs and Shadow's pawprints beside mine, it arrived like an ache —small, trembling, real. Not a roar, not a sunrise. A hairline crack in the stone I'd been living under. The first fracture where light could get through.

I've seen hippos vanish beneath the Niger River.

Watched snow kiss rooftops in Switzerland. Eaten couscous in Morocco. Petted cheetahs in South Africa. Heard silence in

Mali and music in Benin. But only here, only here, did the silence feel holy.

Daffodils breaking through the crust of salt. Hope as insurgency. The trail didn't just hold me. It sang my name back into the wind.

Massachusetts isn't just where I live. It's where I was written. And when I asked this place if I could stay, it answered in daffodils and wind:

You already do.

So, I stayed.

Not forward.

Not back.

But into the marrow of the beautiful state I call home.

Into the breath that stayed.

Into the dirt that dared me to rise.

And the trail did not vanish.

It opened.

And the wind did not leave.

It learned my name.

And the dark passenger, for once, walked behind me in silence.

THE LAND THAT NAMED ME

It didn't ask for permission.
It carved my name in frost. In root. In bone.
It held my breath when I had none left.
It silenced the passenger.
It steadied my pulse.
And when I fell, it whispered—not in warning,
but in welcome: Stay.

14

THE NEIGHBORHOOD THAT RAISED ME

Some places don't raise you. They forge you—quietly, like a fire that doesn't speak until it's gone cold. Cary Drive wasn't a neighborhood. It was a ward against the world. It held me before I knew I needed holding.

IT WAS A PROMISED land I hadn't earned—a sanctuary disguised as a cul-de-sac. The woods whispered my name before anyone else did. The fire pit was the first place I learned to belong without explaining why I needed to. And one day, without ceremony, I let go. But it never did.

I didn't know then that one day, I'd build a fire pit just like it in a backyard hundreds of miles away—just to try and summon what I lost here. To reclaim the smoke that remembered my name.

Before the silence, before the collapse, there was laughter through the woods. Cary Drive didn't save me. But it gave me a place soft enough to shatter in.

When we first moved to Massachusetts, I barely cared. My parents had picked the house. I hadn't even seen it. We stayed at the Sheraton in Framingham while the finishing touches were added. But the first time I saw the top-left window, I knew it was mine. It looked out over the woods, and something about its quiet vantage whispered that I'd be safe here—at least for a little while.

The air was brisk. It felt cleaner than what we'd left behind. I remember missing Africa terribly, but something about the way the trees curved over the yard, the way the cul-de-sac lay cradled in the arms of the woods, made me believe this could be home.

The house was a new colonial with a big backyard—big enough for 4v4 soccer matches. There was a storm drain on the property that foxes sometimes visited, and under the deck, a family of rabbits made their home. Our basement became my first stage, my hideout, my bunker. Later, my bedroom.

That street became a cradle. Cary Drive wasn't just my address. It was a living thing, built with laughter and smoke and scraped knees. The houses weren't just structures. They were portals. And I thought—I really thought—we'd stay.

We were the second house built. The Nowitz's, just behind us, were first. Jewish and Danish. Multicultural like us. Gary, their dad, would become one of my most trusted mentors. He had a way of seeing through you without pressing.

Andy lived diagonally across the street, son of the neighborhood postman. We became brothers-in-mischief. Dennis came next—young, wide-eyed, and slowly folded into our lives like a missing piece we didn't know we needed. Josephine, Nina, Dylan. More names, more summer nights.

We had rituals. Hide-and-seek games that sprawled into the woods, camo suits to cheat with. Construction sites became our bases. Treehouse forts were made from scrap wood. And in between all of it—the fire pit.

Every new family that moved in was welcomed like a new tribe member. We shared a community ride-on lawnmower. We helped shovel each other's driveways. The fire pit—shared by three homes—was our sacred ground. Friday nights, it glowed.

One night, I noticed how many of us there were. New kids. Laughter. Someone had brought out a speaker, Jack Johnson hummed through the air. The logs snapped loud. And for a moment, the fire lit up every face, every life braided together in communion. The warmth on my face wasn't just the flames—it was memory being made in real time.

Even the dark passenger stayed quiet that night, lulled by smoke and summer.

That was church.

THE FLAME THAT LISTENS

Some fires were never meant to warm hands.
They were meant to remember names.
Each flicker a vow, each crackle a hymn.
And even now, the ashes whisper what we once were.

Some houses are never haunted. They just remember who you were before the world tried to forget you.

Gary once pulled me aside while I was home from Landmark. I was trimming the lawn, trying not to look like I was crumbling inside. He handed me coffee. Asked how school was. I told him "Okay," which was a lie.

He didn't push, not too hard. Just said: "You're smart. But smarts isn't enough. If you don't finish, the world decides what you're worth."

Stathis caught me sneaking back through Weston Nurseries after getting my car stuck in the snow. I had taken it to do some off-roading. He heard coyotes on the phone and said, "Jesus, Chris. Please don't get eaten." When I told him what I'd done, he offered to pull my car out. He shook his head the whole way to rescue me. "Use your brain next time," he said. "You only get one life."

Some fires die. Others wait. But this one? It still knows my name—and it's daring me to light it again.

There was the red house at the edge of Weston Nurseries.

They nurseries were right through the woods, and we'd bike there. The house, abandoned, we thought. Andy and I poked our heads in one summer. Cobwebs. Silence. We explored it, dubbed it haunted. Later, we brought Dennis there at dusk. Told him legends. Lured him into the basement and ditched him as he descended. Heard his faint cries, panicked. Eventually, we pulled him out. Kids are awful. Boys especially.

THE HOUSE THAT BREATHED

Not all houses sleep.
Some hold their breath for decades,
waiting for the boy who never got to say goodbye.
Every floorboard is a psalm.
Every doorframe hums your name when you pass.

Nina's childhood on Cary Drive was different. As she grew older, she began spending time with kids her age. She was into soccer, into her friends. She didn't always show up at the fire pit. I was drawn to the older ones, to the woods, to the hush of connection outside of school. I think my roots grew deeper because I needed to find a place to feel safe, seen.

Our neighbors were my surrogate family. I lived with Stathis briefly, when I was transitioning from Trinity to Landmark. Visited Jerry Joyce often. Gary's home became sanctuary. When the dark passenger was loud, they quieted him without even knowing he was there.

Months, after Marianne and I separated, I returned. Ava and I went to church in Hopkinton, then walked the old path through the woods to Cary Drive. Someone had installed a granite trailhead and solar path lights. The mailbox I installed with my dad still stood—same cracked plastic flowerpot at its base. But the door was purple. "Yuck," I said. Ava laughed.

No other house has felt like this. Not Kensington, Maryland. Not Fells Point in Baltimore. Not the Cape Cod styled home we bought on the peninsula that cracked under the weight of silence. Only Cary Drive ever knew my name before I did.

THE ROAD THAT REMEMBERS

There is a path that still knows your weight.
The trees lean inward.
The stones hush underfoot.
Even the wind steps aside so you can come home without shame.

I tried to condense a childhood into a walk. It wasn't enough. I pointed out where the fire pit had been. It was still there. Quiet, waiting.

We bumped into the Fezidis family. They said the neighborhood wasn't the same. Some bonds had frayed. Less community. More isolation. But the memory of what had been still hovered in the space between homes.Some homes vanish. Others burn underground, waiting for your return.

And then I remembered a different visit. I had brought Shadow to Cary Drive once. She was younger then. We stayed with the Joyces. As soon as she got out of the car, she crossed the street and laid down in the center of our old yard. Like she'd been born there. Like she knew.

I took a picture. In it, she's sitting up—serious, contemplative. She looks like she's guarding something invisible. She walked like she'd built the place herself. Like the land had called her back. She didn't sniff around like a tourist. She stood in the middle of the yard like a sentinel returned to post.

She had never been here before—but she lay down like she always had. For a moment, I wondered if she wasn't visiting but remembering. And I knew she belonged here. Just like I did. The air seemed to steady around her, as if the earth had been holding her name in silence, waiting to speak it aloud.

Watching her, I felt a strange calm—like the land was reminding me that belonging wasn't mine alone to wrestle with.

She carried it too, without fear, without apology. And in that, she gave me permission to stay.

THE GUARDIAN AT THE EDGE

She walked the yard like she built it.
Like the land itself had called her back.
Shadow did not visit that day— she remembered.
And her memory made the grass sacred.

And I wonder: what if she had grown up here? What if she had raced through these woods with us?

The day we left Cary Drive for good back in 2012, I looked back and whispered, "Thank you." Not to the house. To them. To every neighbor who held a piece of me without knowing they were keeping me alive.

The one totem I took with me was the guitar I bought while the house was still ours. And when I built my new fire pit in Maryland, it was the first sacred thing I added. A replica of holy ground.

You never say goodbye to a place like Cary Drive.

It echoes in every fire pit you build. In every dog that remembers. In the hum of a guitar string when no one's around.

Sometimes, I still hear it—the laughter, the rustle of the trees, the creak of the deck boards as someone carries another chair to the circle.

THE WHISPER THAT WAITS

Some places do not haunt.
They keep the porch light on.
They hum lullabies into the soil and wait for the lost son to return.
Even silence, here, is a form of love.

I didn't get away. Not really. Some ghosts don't rattle chains. They wait with open arms. Cary Drive never let go. It simply stepped into the silence and waited for me to find my voice.

Cary Drive never said goodbye. It didn't need to. It stood quietly, the same way it always had—like it knew I'd return again someday, even if only in memory.

Part Three

THE COLLAPSE AND THE CHOICE

The mask rotted.
The passenger whispered, "you don't have to stay."
The light flickered. My hands reeked of antifreeze. I waited.
She didn't bark. She just stood—Shadow, unmoving.
The sentinel. And death, confused, passed us by.
The crack stayed. So did the dark.
But so did I.

15

THE FEBRUARY REVERSAL

Some knives don't cut skin. They cut silence.

IT WAS the beginning of February 2024. The apartment was too quiet. Not peaceful. It was hollow. Like someone had opened the window to scream and forgot to close it. The kind of quiet that makes your bones ache. Shadow stirred beside me, her head lifting, ears alert. She felt it too.

My breath fogged in the air even though the heat was on. A phantom chill. I rubbed my eyes and rolled toward the blue pulse lighting up the bedroom like a dying star.

Her phone. Buzz. Pause. Buzz.

It was around 5:30 a.m. on a Saturday. I wanted to sleep in. I reached toward her side of the bed, half-asleep—ready to mumble something about silent mode.

But the sheets were still cold. She wasn't there.

I rolled over and reached for the phone. Picked it up just as it buzzed again.

Lilith.

"Can't wait to show you the condos in Maryland in a couple

of days!" Maryland. Condos. Exclamation points—because even betrayal should be chipper.

No conversation. No fight. Just a plan. Made without me. She was leaving.

Her footsteps approached before her voice did.

She saw the screen in my hand. She didn't flinch.

"I was going to tell you," she said.

She wasn't.

The air didn't just go out of the room—it turned on me.

Heavy.

Sharp. I stood there while she explained, but none of it mattered. Not really.

She hated this state.

She hated her job.

She missed the version of her life where I wasn't in it.

"My mom was right," she said. Like gospel.

Right about what? That I was a detour? A blemish? A burden?

We went through the motions after that. Holding hands with fingers like wires. Kissing with closed mouths and held breath. Valentine's Day came. I made the reservation. She wore red. We smiled like trained mannequins.

That night, I told her I still believed in us.

I asked if she did.

She walked into the kitchen. I followed. She turned. Neutral.

"Why don't you just kill yourself?"

Time stopped. The hum of the fridge. The tick of the stove. Everything else held its breath.

Then—she placed a knife in my hand.

Not tossed. Not thrown. Placed.

Her fingers wrapped mine around the handle like a gift.

"You want to die anyway, don't you?"

Her voice didn't rise. It didn't crack. It was a lullaby made of razors.

THE SIREN'S KNIFE
She didn't scream. She hummed.
And her melody said: End it.
She placed the blade in his palm like a sacrament.

The fight carried into the hallway. She said she regretted moving up. That I was to blame. That none of this was what she wanted. And then she walked back into the kitchen, opened the drawer, and grabbed the knife again. This time, she didn't just place it in my hand—she tried to guide it. Pressed her hand over mine. Steered it toward myself. Calm. Steady. Like it was an act of mercy.

Something inside me left. I don't remember what happened after that. Just that I woke up on the couch. Alone. The knife on the floor. Her suitcase packed.

THE ROOM THAT KEPT BREATHING
The walls did not speak.
But they listened.
They still do.

Shadow curled beside me, nose tucked into her chest, her body warm against my feet like she was trying to stitch something back together. Her eyes tracked me as I sat up. No questions. Just presence. Just breath.

The coffee pot was empty. I drove her to the bus stop. It rained like it knew. She hugged me like I wasn't already bleeding.

"I'll always love you," she said. Then she paused and followed it up with a shrug and "Maybe someday."

Then she was gone.

I went back to silence. The apartment turned hostile. Every wall a witness. Every object a traitor. I couldn't breathe in it.

My sister said, "If she comes back, she packs her shit. You're done." She and Marianne had a phone call. Made a plan. When

Marianne returned, she'd have three days to gather everything. No more. No less.

My mom flew in from Ecuador. Shadow stayed close, curling beside me like a sentry made of breath and fur.

Marianne came back to pack her things. She cried. She said she missed me. She asked for me to change my mind.

I stayed at my sister's.

Day two—I saw her. We held hands. We said things. We danced around the edge of maybe.

Then she left. That night I texted her. "Did you get home okay?"

She said yes. Then:"I got a lawyer. I'm filing for divorce."

And just like that—everything collapsed.

I couldn't breathe. I couldn't sit. I couldn't be.

So, I left. I drove.

Bought antifreeze from a gas station with flickering lights. Sat in the car. Watched my hands. Didn't move.

But Shadow. She was waiting. She wouldn't understand.

So, I drove home. Didn't tell anyone. At least not yet.

One week later, in therapy, I cracked.

Told the truth.

So, it got reported.

Cops came.

I told my mom. Told her they were coming.

She went to my apartment to be with Shadow.

They brought me to the ER.

I spent two days in a hospital gown staring at ceiling tiles.

Then to a hospital forty minutes away in Cambridge.

The psych ward.

But that's the next chapter.

This one? This was the unraveling. The bloodless exhale. The silence that bruised.

This was the February Reversal.

The night she placed the blade in my hand like a sacrament.

The night my dog slept beside me like a psalm.

The night my name lost its shape in my mouth.
No one saw the wound.
Because it didn't bleed—it echoed.
And some part of me is still in that room.
Still holding the knife.
Still waiting to be forgiven for surviving.

THE PASSENGER WHO WATCHED

The dark passenger didn't scream that night.
He didn't drive.
He just watched—silent, complicit.
And when I looked in the mirror, he blinked.

16

THE SILENCE THAT BROKE ME

They say resurrection begins with a scream. Mine began with silence. And in that silence, I met the version of myself that survived. Some silences are prisons. Others are altars.

I WOKE up under white lights that hummed like judgment. The kind of light that doesn't just illuminate you—it interrogates. I blinked, but the ceiling didn't change. Still tiles. Still fluorescent. Still sterile. The gown they gave me was thin, itchy, translucent. My skin felt foreign. Like it belonged to someone else.

I didn't know where I was.

But I knew where I wasn't: at home. With her. With Shadow. With anyone.

A nurse came in. Asked my name. I flinched. Said it. It came out like a question I hadn't studied for.

My mother was somewhere nearby. I could feel her worry vibrating through the walls. I asked about Shadow. The nurse told me dogs weren't allowed in this unit. That sentence alone almost broke me.

When the nurse touched my wrist for vitals, I flinched. Not

from fear—but because for one fractured second, I thought it was her hand. Wrapping mine around the blade again.

So, I lay there, suspended in some in-between realm where sound was muffled and time folded in on itself. The ER didn't feel like a place. It felt like a sentence. The silence leaked from the vents. Sat in the corners like smoke. It wrapped itself around me like a mother who didn't know how to love. My mouth tasted like metal. My eyes burned like they had forgotten how to close.

I kept turning toward the sound of nails on tile. But it was just my own heartbeat, clawing to stay.

THE ROOM THAT DIDN'T ECHO
No mirrors. No clocks. Just waiting.
The silence didn't crush me. But it watched.

Two days passed like smoke. I didn't eat. Or maybe I did. I couldn't remember. Everything tasted like shame. I watched the ceiling like it might open and swallow me. The dark passenger didn't speak. He didn't need to. His silence pressed against the small of my back and waited.

The only thing that moved was breath. Mine. Measured. Shallow. Practiced.

I thought of the couch. The knife. Her words. And Shadow's eyes watching me not die. I wanted to disappear just enough to not exist—but not enough to leave her. Not enough to let my mother find my body.

That was the tether.

That thin.

Once, I heard a whisper in the room. Three words: *You're not done.* But when I looked, there was no one. Just the silence, humming.

I thought about calling someone. Just to hear a voice that remembered me without flinching. But what would I say? How do you explain that surviving feels like betrayal?

Then they wheeled me out. Put me in an ambulance. Drove

me to Cambridge. The ride was quiet. City passed in a blur of ice and stoplights. I couldn't stop seeing Marianne's hand over mine. Couldn't stop hearing the sound of a knife sliding across the counter. I could still feel the weight of her fingers. Still hear the lullaby made of razors.

The doors to the ward opened with a hiss. And then closed behind me with a finality that stole the breath from my chest. It was a monastery of broken saints.

There was the Colombian woman. With eyes that looked like they remembered every lifetime she'd survived. A Portuguese-speaking elder who muttered prayers in the hallway. A young man who hummed to himself like it was the only sound that hadn't betrayed him.

One patient never spoke. Just stared. Eyes locked on mine for hours. And then one morning—gone. No explanation. No goodbye.

I didn't speak. Not yet.

She spoke first. The Colombian woman. Her name was Karen.

In Spanish, she asked if I understood.

I did.

She told me she'd been trafficked. That she lost her daughter. That her name was still hers but didn't feel like it. That her silence wasn't fear anymore—it was sacred. She'd learned to listen to what pain said when it didn't have a mouth.

I nodded. My throat burned.

"I'm not like you," I said. "I wasn't strong. I didn't fight."

She turned to me slowly. Her voice was quiet, but it carried weight.

"You survived something no one saw," she said. "That kind of pain is invisible. But it still leaves scars."

I looked at the floor. "I didn't want to die, but I didn't know how to keep breathing."

Karen reached out, gently. Not to touch—just to let her presence bridge the gap.

"We survive by telling the truth," she said. "Even if it shakes. Even if it stutters. Even if it bleeds on the way out."

That silence? It didn't bruise. It blessed.

There was a mirror in the ward. Thick glass. Smudged. The kind meant to keep you from seeing too much. Or maybe just enough.

I stood in front of it one morning. Looked at my face.

It wasn't the same one Marianne left.

I whispered my name. It came out wrong.

I said it again. Louder. It shook something loose. A breath. A thread. A fracture that didn't shatter.

And behind me, just for a moment, I saw something blink. Not me. Not her. Not Shadow. The dark passenger had followed me in.

THE NAME I DIDN'T RECOGNIZE

It wasn't lost.
Just buried.
Under shame.
Under fear.
Under everything I had to be.

There was no miracle. No movie moment where it all came back. Just a slow returning. To my name. To my breath. To the possibility that I could one day feel whole.

I began to participate in everything the ward offered. Group therapy. Journaling circles. Morning check-ins. Art groups. Breath work. I raised my hand. I shared. I tried. Because even if I didn't believe yet, I wanted to. I wanted to want to live. And that was enough for now.

I became known as the one who always showed up. Who listened. Who asked questions. I wasn't healing—I was excavating. Clearing out the wreckage so something else could grow.

The staff noticed. So did the patients. Some even thanked me.

"You remind me that it's okay to hope again," one whispered.

I didn't know what to say. So, I just nodded. Let the silence speak for both of us.

And still—I missed Shadow. Missed the feel of her weight beside me, anchoring me to the world. I still scooted to one side of the bed. Old habit. Hopeful delusion.

But even her absence became a kind of presence. I could feel her. Not physically. But spiritually. As if some part of her refused to leave me. As if she knew I wasn't done yet.

And maybe I wasn't.

THE HAND THAT STAYED

I didn't reach out.
But something held on.
Maybe it was God.
Maybe it was Shadow.
Maybe it was the breath I forgot I still had.

Before I left, they brought me into a small room. No windows. A whiteboard, a clipboard, a therapist, a nurse, and a resident doctor with a pen he kept clicking like a metronome. Together, we crafted a plan. Not a roadmap to healing—just a compass pointing north.

It was simple, but not easy: Intensive outpatient at McLean. Safety check-ins. Medication adjustment. Weekly therapy. Daily structure. Three people I could call. One reason to stay.

I wrote down Shadow's name.

Not as a contact. As a promise.

THE NAME THAT HELD ME

It wasn't a person.
It was a paw print in my chest.
It was the last thread. And I clung to it.

The therapist underlined it twice. "This plan isn't your sentence," she said. "It's your rebellion."

Where once a blade had found my hand, now a pen did. One held endings. The other—beginnings I didn't yet trust.

I turned the page, the ink still wet, and stared at the shaky lines of my own handwriting. They didn't look like mine. They looked borrowed, rehearsed, like a mask trying to become a map. I wanted to believe that scratching words into paper could hold me here. I wanted to believe rebellion could be that quiet. I didn't know how to believe her. But I nodded like I did.

The day they discharged me, I walked out through white hallways that smelled like antiseptic and resignation. The doors didn't slam. They didn't echo. But I still flinched when they shut. The silence on the other side wasn't freedom. It was a test. Every step felt like contraband. Like I had smuggled myself back into the world without permission.

THE THRESHOLD THAT DIDN'T APOLOGIZE
No bang.
No warning.
Just a hush of goodbye pretending it was mercy

I didn't walk out whole. But I walked out. And that mattered. I carried the plan like a flare in my pocket. Something small. Something fragile. But mine.

The passenger didn't scream. But he faded—just slightly—as the words formed on paper. Structure was his enemy. Breath was his betrayal. I carried silence with me—not the kind that wounds. The kind that waits in corners. The kind that hums in the walls. The kind that watches you breathe to make sure you still do. And somewhere inside that silence... I began again.

They say resurrection begins with a scream. But mine didn't. For me, it began with a plan. With stillness that didn't kill me, but held me. It didn't ask for proof.

It just let me live.

17

THE LONG WAY OUT

They handed me a discharge paper and called it freedom. It felt like exile.

THE DAY I left the hospital, the sky was the color of mourning. Rain fell in tired sheets. A cab waited outside with the engine already running. I didn't want to speak to the driver. I didn't want to speak to anyone. I slid into the back seat and let the window blur into memory. Trees passed like shadows. I didn't feel released—I felt unsupervised.

The apartment wasn't a battlefield anymore. But it wasn't sanctuary either. It was the shell of something that had been holy and defiled. I opened the door, and everything inside greeted me like a ghost that still wanted something.

Shadow met me at the threshold. Tail low. Eyes wide. She didn't bark. She didn't flinch. She just stood there, like a sentry carved from silence.

Her mug. Her scarf. The dent in the couch. All still there. The hallway where the knife almost became prophecy. Everything remembered.

THE HOUSE THAT KEEPS THE KNIFE
It watched him return.
It knew he would.
Every door whispered: welcome back to the ruin.

My mother was still in town. She had stayed longer than expected. She cooked. Cleaned. Asked questions. Too many questions. "How do you feel?" "How do you feel about how you feel?" I didn't have language for either. Her care felt like a lecture written in a language I couldn't read.

But I didn't ask her to leave. Her presence, even when too much, was still a flicker of light in the void.

Eliza—my therapist—was the one who truly saw. She had been there since the first breakdown and helping me with autism diagnosis. When I was trying to learn how to live differently. I stopped therapy for a while, thinking maybe I could handle it alone. I couldn't. When things fell apart with Marianne—when Lilith's voice became smoke in my lungs—I returned.

Eliza coordinated everything. With the ward. With the doctors. With McLean. She moved in the background like a sacred architect, laying bricks I wouldn't appreciate until later.

When my family wanted me resurrected overnight, Eliza whispered the myth that saved me: *Recovery isn't linear. It's not a staircase—it's a labyrinth.*

My sister didn't understand. She thought grief had a deadline. "Marianne's gone," she'd say. "You don't have anyone controlling you anymore. You should be better now."

My mom tried to empathize, but her urgency was rooted in guilt. She wanted redemption through my healing. I wanted silence.

Jenny kept calling. Every day. Her voice like a lighthouse I didn't ask for but needed. You'll meet her soon.

When summer came, my mom left. Maybe too soon. Maybe just in time. I still don't know. The apartment was too loud in its quiet. So, I started going outside. Shadow needed the fresh air. So, did I.

We walked the complex. We found other souls. I started showing up at the pool—not to swim, but to feel less invisible. I started drinking. Enough to forget. Enough to silence the memories. It worked, until it didn't.

There was one night. A deeper spiral. I had too much. Everything blurred. I woke up on the floor of the living room with Shadow nudging my face. I didn't know how I got there. My head hurt. My shirt was damp with sweat. Something inside me cracked open like a warning.

That night, I texted Eliza: *"I think I'm slipping."*

She replied: "Then hold onto something. Start small."

That night, I heard him again. The dark passenger

THE LITANY OF THE DARK

You are not becoming.
You are breaking.
You are not walking out.
You are dragging yourself.
They will leave.
They always do.
You are breath without body.
A ghost too scared to vanish.

The next morning, I brewed coffee. Just coffee. The act felt impossible and sacred. I sat on the floor with Shadow and watched the light move across the rug.

It became a ritual.

Every day, same time.

Coffee. Shadow. Stillness.

I remember the first breaths of color that started to come back. It didn't happen all at once.

It began with a sound...the scrape of a chair at the pool, a child's laugh spilling over the fence, a daffodil blooming in the courtyard when it shouldn't.

They were tiny breaches in the gray. They weren't hope. They were proof that hope hadn't been completely burned out.

I started writing again. One sentence a day. Even if it hurt. Especially if it hurt.

THE ALTAR OF THE MUNDANE

One cup of coffee.
One open curtain.
One quiet laugh.
That's what it took to hold the monster back.
Not strength. Not courage. Just ritual.

Some mornings the quiet pressed too hard, and I thought I'd vanish back into it. But then the world intruded in ways I couldn't ignore—the clatter of kids' bikes in the parking lot, the neighbor's dog barking at nothing, the stubborn green of weeds breaking through the pavement. I hated it and needed it in the same breath. Those small interruptions reminded me the world kept moving, even if I hadn't decided whether I wanted to follow.

My sister invited me to gatherings. Cookouts. Sandwiches by the beach. She didn't always understand, but she kept showing up. That mattered.

Jenny visited twice. Her presence reminded me that being seen didn't have to hurt.

My family started to fear anyone I met. "You have to be okay on your own," they said. "People might take advantage." They were right. And they were wrong. Being alone felt like Marianne's echo—sharp, repetitive, unrelenting.

I let go of my health. Gained weight. Stopped caring. I wanted to vanish without dying.

One night I stood in front of the mirror. Shirtless. Pale.

Bloated. I whispered, "You're disgusting," just to see if the reflection would fight back. It didn't.

But I kept my job. Somehow. I even thrived. I told a few colleagues the truth. They responded with more kindness than I thought I deserved. Some still check in. One plays Mario Kart with me.

Work was the only place where I didn't have to explain my breath.

McLean had made recovery sound like a map. Follow this. Get better. But when I left, I was still bleeding in places no one could see. I thought I should be fixed. Eliza said otherwise.

"You're not broken," she said. "You're becoming."

I hated that. I needed her to be wrong.

She never was.

THE MAP WRITTEN IN SCARS
Recovery wasn't a ladder.
It was a maze with your voice scratched into the walls.

One day in group, someone cracked a joke. Another day, my sister sent me a meme. I laughed.

Not because I was okay. But because I wasn't dead.

The laugh didn't erase the darkness. But it brought color back to the edges.

And that, for now, was enough.

I wasn't healed. But I stayed.

I didn't rise. I remained.

I didn't escape the maze. I mapped it with breath.

And in this new mythology—staying was the sacred act.

They handed me freedom. It felt like exile.

But exile, at least, means I lived.

18

THE PAPER THAT CUT

The end didn't come with fire. It came in triplicate. Not all spells are cast in blood—some are signed. Some are sealed. Some wear the face of a form and call themselves freedom.

BY THE FIRST of March 2024, she filed for divorce. One week after she moved her things out of the apartment. Six months after begging me for a second chance.

We were here again.

THE SUMMONING
It wore no face, only a stamp.
No weapon, only ink.
But it knew where I lived.

But this time, it wasn't a warning shot. It wasn't the shaky draft we almost signed in Maryland. It wasn't a maybe. It was real. Filed in Massachusetts. Inescapable.

I wasn't ready.

I scrambled to find a lawyer. I needed someone who didn't

just know divorce law—I needed someone who understood ghosts. Trauma. Neurodivergence. The weight of love turned weapon.

I interviewed several until I found one who saw me—not just my case. I gave him everything. Even the postnuptial agreement she and I had drawn up during the false reconciliation just five months before.

He built a team. They built a strategy. The pen they gave me was black, ordinary. But I knew—it had killed a future once. And every time Marianne's lawyer replied, I collapsed. I panicked. I melted.

But they didn't. They stayed grounded when I floated off the edge. They brought me back every time.

Just before that second filing, there had been the first attempt—back in Maryland. It started back in September of 2023. She had refused to sign the agreements. She kept shifting, redrafting, stalling.

The vow didn't die with the marriage. It stayed. It slept in my lungs and woke in my bones. Then she said she missed me. Then she cried. Then she begged.

We were talking every day. She said she'd made a mistake. I believed her. But I didn't trust her. Not without proof. I gave her a plan. Sell the house. Escape the debt. Escape her mother. Move to Massachusetts. Get a job. Commit to therapy. Show me it's different this time.

She agreed. She signed. The Maryland divorce vanished like smoke. We packed up the house together. I found us a new apartment in Plymouth. I went back to the fire.

THE GHOST WHO PROMISED

She said the right words.
But her voice belonged to someone else.
And every syllable smelled like smoke.

Everyone told me not to. Eliza. My sister. My mother. Jenny.

But I was chasing a memory. A comfort. A version of me I hadn't learned to grieve yet.

Some nights I lay awake rehearsing the goodbye I never said. Other nights I rehearsed the return. In my head she still laughed like she used to, still touched my wrist in a way that made the noise stop. Trauma makes ghosts magnetic. I knew the fire would burn me, but I wanted to touch it anyway—if only to feel something familiar.

She didn't walk into the courthouse. She was summoned. This wasn't a separation. It was an unbinding. The kind done with salt, blood, and ink. And I wasn't a man—I was a ghost she once loved, now standing trial for haunting her.

This time, she filed. New court. New case. Massachusetts.

And now, she didn't want to honor anything we'd agreed to. Not the postnup. Not the alimony waiver. Not the debt terms. She wanted more. She told me not to contact her. And I didn't. But the silence echoed.

At first, I was wrecked. Still grieving. Still hoping. Still praying the ghost would turn around and speak. Some things don't shatter. They vanish. Quietly.

But then, something shifted. Jenny. Shadow. Ava. My job. My breath. Every day that passed in silence became a balm. I didn't reach out. I didn't beg. I didn't plead. And slowly... I didn't want to.

THE HALL OF ECHOES

No one screamed.
But everything remembered.
The tiles knew names.
The walls kept vows.
Even silence had a memory.

Months passed and October arrived. A cold rain fell like punctuation. My brother came with me to court. We waited in the corridor until she arrived. She didn't look at me. Not once.

The rain didn't fall. It whispered at the windows like it had secrets I already knew.

In the courtroom, I sat five rows back. Watched her shoulders. Watched the judge speak. Seven minutes passed like a lifetime.

And in my head, I whispered: I forgive you. Not for you. Not to make peace. But because I needed to stop bleeding in your name. Because forgiveness was no longer a gift. It was a closing incantation. A door sealed with ash and breath.

Even the dark passenger stayed quiet. As if this severance was sacred. As if he, too, knew it was over. He didn't blink when the judge spoke. He just nodded, like he'd been waiting for this chapter to end. Just like me, he wanted to hold her accountable.

He whispered, *"You said forever. You wore rings like armor. You carved a life from promises—and now you want to leave? I never wanted us to leave."*

She wanted to go back to Maryland. She told me that the night the knife danced. She never left Massachusetts. Even now, months later, I don't know if she'll ever go. And I don't care.

"You'll thank me one day," she once said. And maybe I will. But not out loud.

I still want closure. I want to tell her what she put me through. Not to blame her. Not to make her feel guilty. Just so she could see. But what difference would it make? Would she pause? Apologize? Change? Would I believe it?

I don't think I care.

Maybe the real closure isn't her understanding. Maybe it's me no longer needing her to.

It wasn't the knife that did it. It was the form, notarized and dated. It bled nothing. But it severed everything. And the wound did not scar—it breathed.

I wish I could tell Marianne: "you carried laughter in, and silence out. You painted over blood with beige. I still hear your name in the floorboards. I was never home—I was evidence."

I walked out of the courthouse. Rain on my jacket. No ring.

No title. No name beside mine. The pen was still in my pocket. I could feel it pressing against my side like a ghost I finally knew how to carry.

THE PAPER THAT CUT
It didn't bleed when it struck.
It whispered in dotted lines.
And it knew my name better than she did.
And for the first time, I didn't feel owned by the story.

I didn't just walk out of a courthouse. I walked out of her shadow. Some things don't shatter. They vanish. Quietly. The wound still breathed. But so did I. And this time, I was the one holding the pen.

Outside the courthouse the rain had turned to mist. Cars hissed past like snakes shedding their skins. My hands shook, but not from panic. The air tasted metallic, like the first deep breath after surgery. For a heartbeat I felt weightless—not healed, but unbound. The paper was still in my pocket, but for the first time it felt lighter than me.

Shadow wasn't at the wedding. She wasn't wanted there. She wasn't at the courthouse either. Maybe because this was something I had to face alone. Even the fiercest companions know when to stay behind.

THE NAME I LEFT BEHIND
She never took it from me.
But I set it down anyway.
And walked out with nothing but breath.

19

THE LANGUAGE OF SURVIVAL

The first laugh after the fall is a dangerous thing—part resurrection, part betrayal.

WHEN I TRULY LAUGHED AGAIN, I flinched. Not just in my chest—but in some deeper place. A place that had gone silent for so long, I wasn't sure it still remembered how to echo. It felt like a betrayal. Like joy was something I hadn't earned.

It happened at my apartment. The joke wasn't even funny. Something about her dog and socks. But it cracked me open. The sound that came out wasn't soft. It was jagged, unfamiliar. Mine.

My chest ached. My throat tightened. I almost apologized.

Jenny didn't blink. She just moved through the moment like it was weather she'd already walked through, unimpressed by storms.

Shadow stood still. Her ears tilted. Watching. Like she'd just seen something sacred move through me.

Back in 2012, just after I got back from Madagascar, I was lost in the hollow of re-entry back to the United States. We had just moved to Kensington, Maryland and I needed someone to watch Shadow. I didn't know anyone. I found her online. Just a name. A number. A risk.

She called back. We met. Fifteen minutes turned into an hour, and I didn't want it to end. She was tall, porcelain-skinned, fit. But it wasn't her beauty that hit me. It was her mouth—sharp, funny, fast. She matched me without flinching.

That became our language: sarcasm as survival. Truth without trigger warnings.

We started hiking every weekend. Billy Goat Trail. Shadow led the way. Jenny brought whatever dogs she was watching. After, we'd go to Fish Taco. Frozen margaritas, sweat still drying on our skin. We laughed. We existed.

It wasn't romantic. It was ritual.

She was like me—dry, dark, direct. But she had this mystic undercurrent. Ayahuasca retreats. Astrology. Silent fasts. She could spend three days in the woods and call it healing. She moved like someone who trusted silence. I always envied that.

I think I started to borrow it.

We had already been friends for about 8 years when the walls cracked with Marianne—when the mask stopped working—Jenny didn't run. I told her about the suicide attempts. About Marianne's mom. About the night I almost left. She didn't shrink.

She said, "I'm glad you're still here. But you're a fucking idiot. You should've called me. Next time, no one else. Just me."

When I told her about the autism diagnosis, she just asked, "So what does that mean now?"

I told her I didn't know. That it explained things. That it scared me.

She shrugged. "You're still the Chris I love. Autistic or not."

She came to Massachusetts. Twice. After the crash. After everything inside me scattered. She didn't bring solutions. She brought herself. Coffee. Her crooked smile. The kind of presence that says: I'm not here to fix you. I'm just here.

The dark passenger didn't leave. He just grew quieter. Like a wolf at the tree line. Watching. Waiting to be needed again.

Jenny never asked for the mask back. She let me speak through whatever voice still worked—sarcasm, silence, or breath.

One morning she made eggs and potatoes. Same recipe Marianne used. The scent hit first. My body remembered before I did. I froze.

Shadow pressed against my leg.

THE BODY THAT REMEMBERED

The scent of ash wears many faces.
Eggs. Bread. A clean kitchen at dawn.
The body doesn't know the difference.
But this time— it chose breath over fear. It stayed.
Even when it wanted to vanish.

Jenny didn't say anything. Just kept talking about her dog or the hike or something unimportant. And it anchored me. The smell passed. The breath came back.

There was a night after she left—just one—where I couldn't find my breath again. The coffee pot was empty. The house felt like a white room again. Sterile. Hollow. And I thought: maybe this is as good as it gets.

Then Shadow nudged my hand. Grounded me.

Sometimes I'd wake up and forget where I was. I'd reach for my phone to call Marianne. Stop myself mid-dial. Not because I remembered. But because I didn't know who I was supposed to be anymore. So, I called Jenny.

THE FAMILIAR THAT STAYED

She didn't speak. She didn't leave.
She didn't ask me to explain.
She pressed her breath into my hand like it was language.
I remembered how to stay.
Because she never left.

My body remembered how to stay. My family showed up too. They brought logistics. Pill organizers. Doctor's notes. Deadlines. They meant well.

But they carried guilt—for not seeing the signs, for trusting Marianne, for not protecting me.

They wanted me healed yesterday. And in their urgency, I became the one holding their sorrow while drowning in my own.

I don't think they meant to make it about them. But grief doesn't care about intention.

Jenny brought something else. She brought offerings—coffee in one hand, lemons in the other. She didn't ask how I was. She just placed the mug down like communion.

"Drink," she said. And I did.

THE ORACLE IN LEMON LIGHT

She didn't use spells.
Didn't need smoke or sacred words.
She just sliced lemons and spoke like silence was listening.
And somehow, my body heard her.
Not in logic. Not in command. But in breath.

"You don't have to earn staying alive, you know." She said it while drying a plate. Like it was just truth. Like I was the only one who didn't know it yet.

"You know," she told me once, putting milk in a cup of coffee, "your body already knows how to come back. You just forgot how to listen."

Shadow rested her head on Jenny's knee like she knew. Like she trusted her before I did. Like she understood the sound of home returning.

Laughter returned in pulses. Not all at once. But enough to remember its shape.

This wasn't healing. This was remembering.

She didn't pull me out of the dark. She sat beside me until I forgot I was still inside it.

She brought back scaffolding—not just presence, but pattern. Little things.

"Plan your day," she'd say. "Like you used to."

She helped me sort the chaos into buckets: what matters now, what can wait, what was just noise. Structure came back slowly—like breath after drowning.

My work—God bless them—let me unravel and come back on my own terms.

After McLean, I picked up the pieces. Started working again.

Finance for U.S. Government projects doesn't care how you feel—it just cares about the deadline.

In a strange way, that helped. The pressure gave my mind something to do besides spiral.

I was still working from home, though. The walls remembered too much. At first, it was like shouting into a canyon—emails, numbers, calls, all echoing back at me in silence.

I tried to fill the gaps with grocery runs, solo walks, anything to trick my body into thinking I had a life again.

Things got lighter when Jenny came to visit.

Things got better when I met Eva.

That summer, something shifted. I still worked full-time, still hit deadlines, still ran the spreadsheets and delivered the numbers.

But now, the hours after work had color. Adventure, even.

Jenny wasn't the only one holding me up. But she was the only one who didn't ask for a version of me that didn't ache.

We all need pillars. Not just the ones who carry weight—but the ones who stay when we collapse.

Jenny always saw the version of me I hadn't yet become. She never forced it—but she pointed to it constantly, like someone naming a constellation I hadn't noticed in my own sky.

She'd send me links on Instagram about self-improvement and remind me to bring my guitar to the porch. When I didn't want to move, she texted me about getting outside, even if it was just to walk Shadow. She made me laugh while encouraging me to play pickleball and told me to cook my own damn food instead of eating cereal for dinner again.

When I was spiraling, she didn't try to fix it. She just held up a mirror that said: You're still here. So, act like it.

Not by pushing. By reminding.

I didn't always listen. But I always heard her.

And that's what made her different.

THE LANGUAGE OF LAUGHTER

Laughter is a spell that only works if it's broken.
It stumbles out of the mouth like a mistake.
But once it lands—it becomes breath again.
Not medicine. Not cure.
Just proof. She didn't pull me out.
She just stayed long enough for the sound to return.

Shadow curled at my feet. Jenny moved through the kitchen, humming something tuneless. The smell of lemon. The light. The not-quite silence.

I wasn't healed. I wasn't destroyed.

Just... here. Breathing.

The dark passenger didn't vanish. But his voice felt farther now. Like he'd stepped outside to wait in the cold. And for once, I didn't open the door.

And this time, the breath belonged to me.

The breath did not return like a gift.

It returned like a relic—dug from ash, still warm from the fire.

20

THE SILENT SENTRY

Some guardians do not speak. They watch. They stay. Every myth has a sentinel. Mine came with fur, not flame. And when my story forgot itself—she remembered.

SHADOW ENTERED my life long before the collapse. A German Shepherd pup with eyes too wise for her age and a coat that shimmered like dusk. I got her in 2012 while working in Madagascar, thinking I was just adopting a dog. I didn't realize I was recruiting a guardian.

She didn't approach. She arrived. A slow, deliberate drift into the space between my knees, like she'd been sent—like she'd always been meant to find me there, cross-legged and hollowed out beneath a Malagasy sky.

She looked up at me, exhaled like she'd been carrying something heavy, and smiled.

Some dogs are adopted. Others are assigned. By what, I don't know. But Shadow wasn't a coincidence. She was a reply.

Less pet and more incantation—something whispered by the

universe the moment I cracked. She wasn't trained. She was summoned.

She flew back with me, a reluctant immigrant like me, landing in a world neither of us was bred for. But she adjusted. She watched. She learned my moods faster than I did.

And when the world cracked like a ribcage and let the dark pour in, she didn't flinch. She stepped into the fracture and stood like myth.

THE GUARDIAN WHO DIDN'T BLINK

She didn't speak in warning barks.
She didn't howl.
But she knew.
She knew the shape of grief, the scent of danger, the taste of despair.
And she stayed anyway.

When Marianne left, Shadow was the only heartbeat in the room that didn't carry judgment. She didn't ask questions. She didn't offer platitudes. She just stayed. Breathing. Present. She followed me from room to room, like she didn't trust the walls to hold me up.

When I was staring too long at nothing, she'd nose my hand. When I couldn't sleep, she curled beside the bed like a guard at a tomb. When I wanted to disappear, she blocked the door.

She never cared what I lost. She cared that I stayed.

THE DOG WHO STOOD BETWEEN

She stood between the knife and my name.
Between the silence and the scream.
She stood. And didn't move.

Shadow became my tether. In the months after the split, when grief made gravity feel like a choice, she was the thing that kept me grounded.

Not with grand gestures, just with presence. Just with weight.

Just with the soft sound of her paws pacing when my breath faltered.

The dark passenger fed on silence. Grew fat in the quiet between collapse and breath.

But Shadow? She was the firewall. The ward. The one who stood between the whisper and the act. She never looked at him directly. But she knew where he lived.

In the shadows I cast. In the pauses between words. In the mornings I couldn't rise. She would stare into corners like she saw him pacing—and some part of me believed she did.

THE SENTINEL AND THE SHADE

She saw the shade I carried.
Not with fear. Not with judgment.
She stared through him, and he blinked.
He hovered. She held.
He whispered. She breathed.
And every time I almost answered his call—
She nudged me back to earth.

The night I almost vanished, she blocked the door. She didn't growl. She didn't bark. Just stood there, tail low, ears forward, eyes locked on mine. And in her silence, I heard it: *Stay.*

I couldn't even use the bathroom without her stationed outside the door, whining softly, as if the silence might swallow me whole if she wasn't there to bark it away.

THE WARDEN OF BREATH

When I forgot how to inhale, she laid her chest on mine.
We synced. That was the spell.

She became the reason I left the apartment. Because she needed walks. Because she deserved air. Even when I didn't.

I met neighbors because of her. I made friends because she

introduced me first. She cracked open a door I didn't know I had sealed.

She doesn't speak. But she never needed to. Her loyalty was a language. Her eyes, a mirror. A compass. A reason.

Now she's thirteen. Slowing down. Limbs stiff. Eyes cloudy in the morning. But she still follows me, still waits outside the bathroom, still rises when I rise—however hard it gets.

But I remember when she was younger. The ball chasing, the runs through the woods, the endless hours at the park fetching.

Now it's a far cry from that. She's old, she's stiff. I have to carry her up and down stairs, help her on the couch or to get in the car. But she can still walk a bit, and we do.

We go to parks still, she sniffs around, returns to my side.

We both carry the cost of returning. She did not wither. She weathered.

THE FAMILIAR

Not every spell needs words.
Some need only breath, and fur, and eyes that do not look away.

I don't know how much time we have. But I know she gave me more than I can name.

She was the first reason I stayed.

Not for faith. Not for family. Not even for myself.

For her. Because she needed me. Because I needed her.

Shadow doesn't understand the word recovery. She understands rhythm. Proximity. Love without condition.

Her faith in me was never questioned. Not once. Not even when I broke.

And now, in this new chapter—this breath I was never supposed to take—she's still beside me. Still silent. Still watching. Still guarding.

She is the oldest part of my healing.

And the most sacred.

THE BREATH THAT OUTSTAYED THE END
She was born of dusk, but she stayed for every sunrise.
She outlasted the storm, the silence, the sorrow.
And when her breath one day ceases, mine will still echo hers.
Because I learned how to stay from a dog who never left.

She taught me how to stay. But more than that—she taught me how to return. And some nights, when I forget who I am, I listen for her breath.

It always finds me.

THE HOUND OF ASH AND BONE
She did not speak.
She watched. Waited. Guarded.
She knew his breath better than I did.
And when the world fractured, she stepped between me and the dark.
She did not bark. She did not run.
Because love does not always arrive with words.
Sometimes, it arrives on four legs, with eyes full of myth and a silence that saves.

She is slower now, her breath shallower, her steps hesitant. But she is still here.

Still guarding the silence like it matters. Like I matter.

And when her breath goes quiet—if it does before mine—I will still listen for it. Because sometimes, what stays isn't the body. It's the vow.

THE DOG'S PRAYER
He doesn't know that I watched him dream of ending.
He doesn't know that I stood guard through nights that bent him backwards.
I saw him lost in the mirror. I saw the blade. I saw the grief.
But I never saw him as broken.
I only saw him as mine.

There will come a day when the silence outpaces her breath. When the space by the door remains empty. When the paws that followed fall still.

But I will not forget the sound of her presence. I will not unlearn what she taught me.

Because even when the body is gone—the sentinel remains.

In the dust of the trail. In the hush before sleep. In the moment I choose to stay.

She'll be there. Not barking. Just watching.

Invocation Echo – The Last Breath

Some guardians do not leave.
They just become the wind in the hallway.
The shadow in the light.
The reason you keep breathing when you forget how.
Every myth ends—but the sentinel?
She lingers.

21

THE GIRL WHO STAYED

Some stories start with a beginning. This one starts with a weight. Not a memory. A presence.

SHE LOOKED like a secret the sun wasn't supposed to touch. And I should have known—anything that beautiful doesn't stay.

"You don't eat," I said. And in that moment, I wasn't sure which one of us I was trying to save.

"Neither do you," she murmured. "You just starve differently."

I wanted to argue. To tell her I'd eaten yesterday. Or was it the day before?

But I didn't. Because she wasn't wrong.

That was the first conversation that felt like bloodletting. Nothing dramatic. Just slow honesty leaking between words.

If you've come this far, I won't ask you to understand her. Just stay. Like she did.

I met Ava on a day that didn't know it was going to matter. She was visiting a mutual friend at the complex. Nothing scandalous—just a casual hang. I saw her sitting at the pool with our friend, laughing about something I couldn't hear.

And I don't know what possessed me, but I walked over and said,

"Can I join you? Can y'all spare a little concrete for this guy?"

She smirked. Tilted her sunglasses.

And the answer was yes.

She lived in town, in a quiet little neighborhood tucked away in West Plymouth— the kind of street where porches still meant something, where dogs barked like they knew your name.

It reminded me of my old neighborhood in Ashland. That unspoken normal I thought I'd forgotten how to want.

She worked from home, like I did. I was piecing together finance work and memoir fragments. She was processing Medicare claims, if I understood right— a job she downplayed like it didn't matter, but still talked about with quiet competence, like it did.

It started at the apartment pool. Just a glance, a few words, a goodbye she never followed through on. She said she had to leave soon. She stayed.

And we talked for hours. Not about anything big. Not yet. But the kind of conversation that feels like someone just handed you your own name for the first time. My real one. The one I buried to survive.

Just the kind of nothing that feels like a doorway left open, like maybe someone forgot to close it.

Music that wrecked us. The foods we missed from childhood.

How she was in going to rap school because she found lyricism fascinating.

How I was thinking of writing a piece of theater built entirely out of puns. A sort of play on words.

We continued to sit by the pool behind my apartment late afternoon as the blue was slipping into gold, like the light forgot it had somewhere to be.

The water didn't move. Neither did we. We weren't touching. But I swear something was.

She tilted her head when I spoke—like she was tuning into a frequency no one else had ever caught.

She didn't flinch when I paused. Didn't rush to fix the silence. Just let it hang between us like a question I hadn't asked yet.

It wasn't the words. It was the way she looked at me while I said them. Like I wasn't broken glass. Like I'd never been.

We met in the quiet. But we stayed for the storm. And part of me already knew. I wouldn't walk out of this the same.

A couple of days after we met, we'd planned to go see the Michael Jackson musical. We didn't. We ended up sitting by the water, and planned to go another time. Life kept slipping sideways. And somehow, even joy got rescheduled. Now, every time I see the poster, I wonder if she would've danced in the aisle. Or just mocked the lighting choices.

THE SPARK SHE LEFT IN ME

She didn't heal me.
She didn't fix the wreckage.
She lit it on fire.
And danced in the smoke.
She told me I looked good in ruin.
And I believed her. That's what scared me the most.

Our love story wasn't some Instagram-filtered romance. It was cracked screens and loud audio. It was messy. Honest. Human. I brought baggage—not the cute kind with wheels. The kind with broken zippers and emotional booby traps. I flinched from joy because I thought it was bait. I handed her pieces of me like they might bite her.

But Ava didn't flinch. She didn't run. She stayed. She rooted for us. Even when I didn't know how. Even when I thought love was a trick door.

And she did all of it while decimating my dad jokes. She hated them. But she had a favorite: "I'm glad the crowbar was invented because otherwise crows would have to drink at home." That one got a full-body laugh. The kind where she covered her face and said, "I hate that I laughed at that." The rest? She looked at me like I'd insulted her ancestors, her dog, and the concept of humor itself.

Whenever I said something sweet—or made a terrible joke—she'd roll her eyes and say, "Shut up, Richard. Nobody likes a Richard." She got it from *Tommy Boy*. It was her way of pretending I annoyed her. Which meant she liked me. Maybe even loved me.

She left me one note on a napkin stained with iced coffee: "You're exhausting. But I'm still here...too bad your ex couldn't see how fun you are." I folded it and kept it in my wallet. It's still there.

She always lost her keys. Was super messy. Sometimes sang off-key on purpose. Wore sarcasm like sunscreen. She once tried to argue with a customer service bot and won.

She danced while brushing her teeth in my hoodie—too big for her frame, sleeves swallowed in her palms. She burned toast and called it "crunch-therapy." Her humming filled the apartment long after she left. It still does.

She ordered drinks like she was negotiating a hostage situation. Had a laugh that could shatter glass—and a sigh that could level buildings. She was part goddess, part gremlin. An oracle in ripped jeans. A siren who hated mornings and believed glitter was a personality trait.

She didn't just wear glitter. She weaponized it. I'm convinced her soul leaves behind sparkles the way saints leave relics. I still find it on my clothes. That's how I know she's haunting me properly.

The first time I saw her sing, the mic squeaked. She rolled her eyes at it like it owed her money. Then she sang.

Not to impress. To survive.

She didn't belt. She didn't beg. She just opened her mouth and told the silence it couldn't have her. Someone at the bar whispered, "Damn." And I wanted to say, "I know."

"You're not mysterious, Richard. You're just quiet and dramatic," she once said while stealing some tuna off my plate.

Then she added, "But don't worry. I like dramatic. Just not brooding. Brooding is for Batman."

When I told her I thought I was subtle, she laughed: "You're about as subtle as a glitter bomb at a funeral."

She rooted for everyone with the kind of loyalty that made you believe maybe, just maybe, you were worth the chaos. Even when she couldn't believe in herself... she still believed in you.

That—if I'm honest—is what broke me. Because she never saw herself the way we did. So I made it my mission to reflect her.

Not to fix her. Just to hold up a mirror and whisper, "You are not a burden. You are so loved."

She brought peanut butter cups when I was low.

She also left handwritten notes in coat pockets, under pillows, behind my toothpaste.

She once wrote: "I love you more than I want to strangle you. #winning. And I mean that with all my heart. But seriously, thank you for putting up with my shit. Your sacrifice doesn't go unnoticed "

Another time I found three in a single day: One in the fridge: "Don't forget to eat. And no, coffee isn't a meal. Moron."

One in my sock drawer: "You're loved. Even when you wear the weird socks."

One under my pillow: "I saw the texts. We'll talk later. (Kidding. Or am I?)"

Her handwriting made even passive aggression feel like affection. She didn't leave notes. She left landmines that bloomed.

THE NOTES SHE HID FOR ME

"I saw your face this morning and forgot how sad yesterday was."
"You're doing your best. It's adorable. Keep going."
"I'm not a morning person, but I like you enough to fake it."
"Yes, I'm still mad. No, you can't fix it with snacks. (...okay maybe snacks.)"
"Don't forget to feed Shadow. And yourself. In that order."
She didn't write notes. She cast spells.
Left proof that someone once saw me—and stayed anyway.

One night, we drove to the beach. One of those spontaneous, late-summer things. We didn't pack anything—just left. Her hair was still wet from a shower, and she sang along to the radio like she didn't believe in consequences.

I thought maybe this is what healing looks like. Wind. Salt. Her bare feet on the dash.

We sat by rustic benches, the fire crackling between us, its heat carving shadows across her face. A bonfire overlooking the water and the super moon—too bright, too close, like it knew our secrets and refused to look away.

"Do you ever feel like your body isn't yours?" she asked.

I nodded before I even understood what she meant.

She pointed to her stomach. "Sometimes I wish I could unzip it and walk out."

I didn't know what to say. So, I reached for her hand. She let me. But she didn't squeeze back.

And then she laughed. That sharp, lovely laugh that always felt like breaking glass.

"God," she said, "we're a mess."

I smiled. But inside, I felt the panic rise like tidewater.

She touched my face like I might disappear. I flinched anyway.

Not because I didn't want her to. But because she saw me. And I wasn't used to that.

I told her about the bathroom floor. About the night I didn't want to wake up. About Shadow, and how her breath was the only thing louder than the static in my skull. She didn't ask questions. She just said: "I'm glad you're still here."

That was it.

And it meant everything.

Then she whispered: "Me too."

And I didn't ask what she meant.

We talked about her demons. She was frank—blunt, even. Called it what it was.

But when we were out, I didn't want to seem like I was the only one eating. I didn't want her to feel observed. Measured.

So I paid attention. Noticed that when I ordered fish and salad, she'd sometimes pick off my plate. Quietly. Casually. Like it didn't count if it wasn't hers.

I started ordering it every time. Even when I didn't want it. Just so she might eat something.

Not because I thought I could save her.

But because that was the only way I knew how to try. Because part of me understood that wanting to stay broken can feel safer than risking being put back together wrong.

We loved each other like soldiers after a war. Cautiously. Desperately. Quietly.

She was sharp. I was distant. We didn't mean to hurt each other. But sometimes we did.

Still, she never used silence as a weapon. Never used love as leverage.

She was the first new person who looked at me and didn't flinch. And I wanted to be enough for her.

But I wasn't sure how to be enough for myself.

And sometimes, we laughed. Real, stupid, sunlit laughter. Over burnt pancakes. Over dog hair on black shirts. Over the fact that we both knew we were haunted and still kept reaching anyway.

I never said the right thing about her illness. I didn't know what the right thing was.

But I stayed.

And she let me.

That's the part I still think about.

She remembered every bruise. Every skipped meal. Every compliment that sounded like control.

She told me once she didn't believe in happy endings.

I told her I didn't either.

But I believed in her.

And when she reached for my hand in the dark—just once, without flinching—I believed maybe that was enough.

Not forever.

Just enough to stay.

Just enough to breathe.

She showed up on my birthday with a dozen mismatched balloons. They didn't need to match. I kept them until they sagged to the floor, like tired prayers. One of them said *"Congrats Grad."* I think she grabbed it on purpose.

I disappointed her more than once. Especially at Christmas.

My family didn't approve of us. Said I wasn't ready for a relationship. That I needed more time. So, I didn't stay long at her place. I showed up, smiled, left too early. And she smiled back— but it didn't reach her eyes.

That night, she stopped by. Just for a moment. To drop off gifts.

One was a Ferrari experience—eight laps, because she knew I needed to feel velocity again. The other was a card that said: "Running out of Fa La La La La's."

Inside, she'd written: "This isn't the Christmas I pictured. But maybe love isn't perfect. Maybe it's just choosing someone anyway. I love you anyway."

I read it twice. I could feel the disappointment curling between the lines like static. But I could also feel the grace.

She forgave me. Even when I didn't know how to forgive myself.

We were at Pins. Bowling, arcade, karaoke. She convinced my

very karaoke-averse roommate to sing. He butchered "Total Eclipse of the Heart." There is footage. It will outlive us all. Ava filmed it, laughed so hard she wheezed, then leaned in and whispered, "Don't you dare post that. But, also, absolutely post that."

Then she took the mic and sang something completely wrong for her range, on purpose, and still made the room hers. Not because she was the best—but because she believed in the song. And that kind of belief? It's contagious.

THE SECOND VERSE

I don't sing because I'm healed.
I sing because she once stayed to hear me try.
And that's what love sounds like.
Trying again.

The last time she sang, her voice cracked on the first line. She laughed. Then started over. Not for applause. Just to prove she could still defy the quiet.

I wasn't perfect. I was haunted. I was trying. And still—she stayed. She let me stay. And I didn't know how to leave. I didn't want to either.

THE GRIEF THAT LAUGHS

I still hear her laugh when the pain spikes.
Like she knew sorrow would overstay its welcome.
So she left her voice behind—
a weapon I forget I'm allowed to use.

Weeks after she passed, I found a note tucked behind my winter coat. "You looked tired yesterday. Don't forget you're still my favorite idiot." I held it like breath. Didn't cry. Just sat on the floor and let silence fill the room like incense.

I wish I'd told her sooner that I believed in her more than I believed in God.

I went back to the dock. The one where her lips first

touched mine, and time flinched. The wind tasted like her absence—salt and almost. I dropped a note into the tide. It said: *I remember.* The ink bled like prayer. The current didn't carry it. Even the sea wants to keep her.

Shadow used to curl up beside her like she was sacred ground. She'd scratch behind her ears and say, "You're lucky I like your human." Shadow still checks the door sometimes. Like she might be late but not gone.

We met in late June of 2024, just two and a half months after I walked out of McLean—shaky, stitched together with quiet promises. I was still learning how to breathe without apology.

THE GIRL WHO STAYED ANYWAY
She saw the panic behind my eyes and didn't flinch.
She held the sharp parts of me and called them intentional.
She saw the mess and said, "Leave it. Sit with me."
She wasn't perfect. But she stayed.
And maybe that's the most divine thing love can do.

She was light wrapped in laughter; sarcasm folded into sweetness. We hit it off instantly—like two old souls picking up a conversation from lifetimes ago.

Within days, we were celebrating the Fourth of July together. Fireworks exploded over the water. She kissed me like the world was finally safe.

But the world was already counting the days.

We dated through my mess-ups, my recoveries, my flinching from joy. We entered 2025 with plans—summer adventures, a Ferrari drive, road trips with no map. She even helped me reclaim Valentine's Day—the day that, a year before, the knife had danced with Marianne. This time, there was chocolate, sarcasm, and a kiss that didn't ask for anything in return.

By March, we were dancing through St. Patrick's Day at our favorite winery. Her earrings blinked like a disco in mourning. She mentioned a sore throat. Just a cold, she said.

The days blurred after that. She'd feel okay, then not. The night I remember most was a Thursday.

I called after work. "Do you want to come over before karaoke?"

"Maybe," she said. "I might go with you tonight."

When she arrived, her smile looked tired. Her eyes didn't hold their usual defiance.

"I'm not really feeling too good," she said. "My back and head hurt so bad."

I gave her aspirin. A heating pad. Asked her to lie down. She did—but only for a moment. Then sat up and said she wanted to go home. I offered to drive her. She insisted on her car. She was always so damn stubborn.

"Call me when you get there," I said.

She did.

The next day, I called to check in. Her voice was a ghost of itself.

"Call off work," I told her.

"Nah," she said. "I gotta work."

Later that afternoon, she told me she'd been curled up in bed since noon. She asked me to take her to urgent care.

"I need fifteen minutes," I said.

But she decided to have her mom take her instead.

The last text I ever got from her said she was being transferred to the ICU because she had pneumonia.

While she was in the ICU, I didn't want to overstep. I wasn't family. I wasn't next of kin. Just the person who loved her. Loudly. Quietly. Constantly.

I checked in every day—sometimes too many times. Texted her mom. Waited for updates. Prayed in ways I didn't know how.

I visited. Maybe too much. Maybe too little.

I kept wondering what counted as "enough" when someone you love is vanishing by degrees.

I just didn't want to make it harder for them. And I didn't want to leave her alone.

On that fateful Sunday, roughly three weeks after she went to the ICU, my phone buzzed. I stared at the message until my phone dimmed. I wanted to reply. But what do you say to a silence that's already begun swallowing someone? What do you tell a loving parent after they've made the hardest decision of their lives?

On my last visit—just three days before she passed—she seemed better.

There was hope. Not loud hope. Not foolish hope. Cautiously optimistic hope. Just enough to breathe again without guilt.

She was still on the ventilator, but she opened her eyes four times while I was there. Not wide. Just enough to say: *I'm still here.*

I talked to her. Told her what was happening with me. That I was writing a book. That I missed her sarcasm. That Shadow missed her too.

I told her to get better.

Because we still had so much left to do.

I didn't know that was the last time I'd see her awake.

She was on a ventilator for three weeks. No songs. No glitter. No eye rolls to tell me I was still hers.

She passed on April 13th, 2025. No music. No thunder. No do-over. Just a room that dimmed too quickly. Just a world that didn't kneel.

I carry her in that silence. And I carry her every time I wonder if I showed up enough.

One memory bleeds into the next, the way grief rearranges time.

We fought once—hard. I don't even remember what started it. Something small that got big fast. I was projecting. She raised her eyebrows. Then she walked out. Said she needed space.

Two hours later, I found a note taped to my door: "Don't apologize yet. I'm still mad. But I left you soup in the fridge.

And next time, I'll post it on your forehead if you fall asleep on the couch again."

She wasn't perfect. She was better. She knew how to love people even when she was disappointed. Especially then.

And she stayed anyway.

Somewhere, I still hear her: "Don't make this poetic, Richard. Just miss me."

THE GIRL WITH GHOST BONES

She was not made. She was conjured.
Drawn from smoke and sea-foam,
stitched with song and spite—
a hymn carved into human skin.
She wasn't a wound. She was the scar that stayed.
The burn that turned sacred.
The laugh that cracked grief open.
She left fingerprints in thunder.
Graffiti on the bones of fear.
Notes in places no one else thought to look.
Now that she's gone, the dark is too quiet.
Because no one sings to it now.
Not like she did.

She left the world mid-sentence. And I've been trying to finish the thought ever since.

I still reach for my phone. The last message I sent her just said, "How are you?" She never answered.

I till expect her voice. Still imagine her groaning at my outfit or my terrible dad jokes with a smirk and a sarcastic gold star. I wasn't perfect. I brought ghosts. But she stayed and loved me anyway.

Now I carry her. In songs. In punchlines. In the silence her favorite chair still holds. In the forgiveness I try to offer strangers because she taught me how. She brought joy into rooms like she didn't believe she deserved to be in them. She lit people up—baristas, servers, cousins, karaoke regulars—then shrunk when the light turned back toward her.

She told me once she didn't think she deserved love. She said it in a whisper, like a confession she'd already been punished for. But she was wrong.

She was joy with teeth. The kind that shows up in someone's worst moment and makes them laugh anyway.

She was empathy with a megaphone and sarcasm with a heart.

She was love. In all its inconvenient, sacred, ridiculous forms.

I carry her like a vow I never got to say.

Like a hymn I hum when the grief gets too loud.

Like fire.

And her name is carved into the soft place behind my ribs. She left the world mid-sentence. But I breathe like she is the comma. And I carry her.

Like a name.

Like a hymn.

Like a fire.

THE NOTE I NEVER GOT TO LEAVE
I was going to write back.
Say something stupid. Say something true.
Leave a card in your jacket,
just like you did in mine.
But I waited.
And now the pocket's still empty.
And the silence knows.

I had the card already. One of those cheesy ones with glitter hearts and a stupid pun. "I appreciate that you don't ever ask me to do things involving early mornings, sweating, or people."

I was going to write: "You make even the bad days feel like they're worth showing up for."

But I didn't write it. I thought I'd have more time.

That I could just find the perfect time to sneak it in her purse.

THE FINAL IMAGE

The mic is still warm.
The room hums like it remembers her.
And somewhere, someone is about to sing the wrong note—too loud, too late, too real.
I hope she hears it.
I hope she rolls her eyes.
I hope she forgives me.
I hope she laughs.
Because the silence misses her voice more than I do— and I didn't think that was possible.

I drove past the gas station where we once bought a Fresca
and she called it "a crime against fruit."
I remembered that. I laughed. Out loud.
Then pulled over. because the tears came too fast to bargain with.
There's no logic to it—what breaks you. A street name. A dumb song. A license plate that ends in 13.
The world keeps spinning.
But she's still there—in the static between songs.
In the click of the turn signal.
In the grief that waits beneath green lights.
She keeps finding me.
In all the places I thought I was safe.
For Valentines Day, I got her a scratch off adventure kit that we could do together all over Massachusetts so that we could go on roadtrips across the state. I haven't opened it yet. But I do know, when I do, it'll be when I have a new friend eager for adventure, and Ava will be with me because I'll carry her in my heart.

THE ECHO I BREATHE THROUGH

She left in the middle of the song.
Not a silence—a pause.
Now the wind carries her name like smoke.
Now my lungs carry her fire like breath.
And the hush between verses still waits for her return.
Not because it expects her—but because it remembers
how the world burned when she sang.
Some nights, I still sing to the dark.
Not because it listens.But because she once did.
And sometimes, in that hush,
I still hear her say—"You're off-key, Richard."
And I sing anyway.

Sometimes I remember the playlist she made for me—titled: *"Songs That Go Too Hard for No Reason."* She said it was a mix of bangers and emotional warfare. It had everything from 2000s emo anthems to that one Miley Cyrus song she said was secretly profound. I still listen to it in the car. And yeah, I still skip track seven. Because that was her favorite. And sometimes loving her now means hitting 'next' before I break.

And sometimes, in that hush, I still hear her say— "Shut up, Richard. Nobody likes a Richard."

Which is how I know she stayed anyway.

And I smile. Because that's how I know she's still here.

THE TENDERNESS THAT SURVIVED

Love knocks like a stranger.
I open the door with a knife in my hand.
She walks in anyway.
I was afraid to be loved,
because I thought love was the thing that burned me.
She cupped my face in both hands,
and said, "This is not a fire.
This is a breath."

22

THE ONE WHO CAME FOR ME

Some rescues don't come with sirens. They arrive in silence—white SUVs at dawn, sisters with steady eyes, dogs that refuse to look away.

MY SISTER NINA didn't ride in with armor. She rode in with a quiet kind of fury—the kind that doesn't burn out.

Nina doesn't flinch. Not when I weep. Not when the house is too silent. She once walked into a storm without an umbrella and said, "it's just water." That's who came for me.

Nina today is nothing like me. She is someone who doesn't show weakness very much. She's the type of person who doesn't let anything get in her way. She achieves everything she sets her mind to. Almost stoic. I'm sure there were days where she broke down and let herself feel. I just haven't seen many of them.

She's never been quiet. Always had friends, played sports, the female version of a jock. But wherever we ended up, she was always my first friend. We're roughly eight years apart.

I remember when she was born. I was almost eight. I showed up at the hospital with all my toys ready to play. My older brother was seventeen by then—too cool for me. But Nina? She was new. She was mine.

THE CALL THAT BROKE THE SPELL

It wasn't a scream. It was a sentence.
Simple. Stern. Alive.
"Pack a bag."
Not a suggestion. Not a question.
A spell cast in three words.
And just like that, the door cracked open.
The dark passenger stirred.
Hope flinched, but it stayed.
Some rescues don't roar. They whisper.
But this one struck like thunder on still water.
Not loud. Jus true.

It was early fall when the second time Marianne asked for a divorce cracked open the floor. The silence between us had turned toxic—thick with the kind of quiet that didn't just fill rooms, it choked them. And I had begun disappearing again. The mask slipping. The dark passenger stirring.

By now, I had told Nina and my mother that I'd attempted suicide—twice—the year before. I told them it was because of the abuse. I told them I was in therapy now.

That I was trying.

But I was losing.

Marianne's second demand for divorce hit like a whispered curse. There were no screams, no plates thrown, just a sterile, soul-splitting undoing. And the abuse, though muted, hadn't stopped. It wore new costumes—avoidance, apathy, entitlement. I felt myself fading.

I texted Nina.

"I don't know how much longer I can hold on."

The reply came like a crack of thunder over still water.

"Chris, it's time. Pack a bag, pack up Shadow's things. I'll be there by morning."

I didn't ask her to come.

Not out loud.

But she came anyway.

THE SISTER WHO ARRIVED

She didn't knock down the door.
She didn't shout my name.
She crossed the border between silence and salvation
With her foot on the gas and her jaw set like stone.
She did not ask if I wanted saving.
She came anyway.
And the dark passenger blinked.

Nina had driven the day before from Massachusetts. She stopped at a hotel to rest. She texted me the next morning, "I am on my way."

I told Marianne that I'd be gone for a couple of weeks. That maybe some time in my home state would help me. I packed accordingly. She left for work like it was just another Tuesday. I put my things outside, waiting for Nina. I walked the neighborhood route Shadow and I used to take.

Shadow's leash in hand, her gait unknowing. We followed the shoreline of the Stoney River, which fed into the Patapsco. It had always been my favorite path.

I didn't know it would be our last. Didn't know the trees would be a memory. Didn't know I'd never look at that river again without hearing the echo of a goodbye I hadn't said.

She arrived and helped me put my bags in.

I talked the entire ride back to Massachusetts, vomiting every word I hadn't dared to say out loud. About Marianne, about the dark. About the nights I didn't make it. She stayed silent. Not cold, just listening. I was terrified, unspooling words like rope trying to tether myself to something real.

She just drove, her hands calm at the wheel, her eyes on the road. The silence didn't judge me.

It held me.

Shadow sat behind me, head rested between the seats, breath warm against my shoulder. She shifted once in a while but never whined. Her presence was a pulse in the quiet- steady, anchoring. I caught her eyes in the mirror once. They were locked on me. Not the road. Not the trees. Just me, like she was counting the words I bled, waiting to see if I'd run out.

The dark passenger rode with us too. He rode shotgun in my chest, silent but smirking. Didn't need a seatbelt. He fed on the static between our words. "*You'll ruin this too,*" he muttered, smug. I kept taking just to drown him out.

"*You talk too much when you're afraid,*" he whispered. But Nina kept listening. Shadow didn't blink. And somehow, the silence didn't cave in.

Nina said nothing. But her silence wasn't empty. It was a rope, and somehow, I kept holding on.

She and Michael took me in. Gave me a room. Gave Shadow a place too. They said I could stay for a year.

Around the same time I bought my house in Maryland, my sister bought a house in Kingston, Massachusetts. Nina's place was an oasis. Woods behind it. A manicured backyard with a pool. Miley, their dog, welcomed Shadow like a cousin. They would play there, swim together. We'd walk the golf course paths just to clear our heads.

But inside?

Nina's house was impossibly white.

The kind of white that didn't welcome dirt, or grief, or anything that couldn't be scrubbed out with a lemon-scented disinfectant. The couch was white. The kitchen was white. The walls, the curtains, the damn coffee mugs—all of it bleached into a kind of sterile calm that felt foreign to my body.

THE WHITE ROOM

Everything was white.
Sofas. Sheets. Silence.
Like grief had been bleached from the walls.
But not from me. Not from her.
So I sat on furniture that didn't understand sorrow
And tried not to bleed on it.

I didn't belong in it. Not the version of me that was fraying at the edges, sleep-deprived, guilt-washed, haunted. Even Shadow hesitated the first night. She stepped through the threshold like a ghost with muddy paws, as if she knew we were trespassing in someone else's illusion of peace.

Nina didn't notice. Or if she did, she didn't comment. She just handed me a towel for Shadow's feet and told me which drawer held the treats.

Everything in her house had a drawer. A label. A place.

And I was trying to figure out if I did, too.

Some nights I'd sit on the edge of the white bed and wonder if she knew how much of me was still scattered. My grief came in shards, unlabelled and sharp, slipping between the tidy drawers she'd built for a life. She never asked where I put it all. She just kept handing me towels and keys, as if she trusted I'd learn my own filing system for pain.

Even the air felt arranged—cool and crisp like it had passed through a filter designed to keep emotion out. My grief didn't know where to sit. My panic didn't know where to echo. And still, I tried not to bleed on anything.

I took my coffee in a white mug and sat in a white chair and watched Nina move through the kitchen like a storm that had been taught to walk quietly. Efficient. Powerful. Contained.

We were so different.

She wore structure like armor. I wore memory like a stain I couldn't scrub out.

She spoke in bullet points. I unraveled in ellipses.

She didn't cry. So I didn't either. But the dark passenger smirked from the corner.

He knew I wanted to.

And still—she made room for me. In her white house. With her white towels and white sheets and white expectations I never quite felt I met.

Even Shadow stayed closer than usual. She'd sit beside the bed, facing the doorway, like she didn't trust the silence not to bite. Some nights I'd wake and find her already watching me. Just watching. As if she had seen this kind of stillness before and knew how easily it could harden into something else.

That first night, I caught her pacing the hallway outside my room. Not restless-, butwatchful. The dark passenger stirred besides me in the sheets and muttered, *"Even your dog doesn't trust this peace."* But I did. Not fully. But I wanted to. And she did too, in her own four-legged way.

I wasn't used to this kind of calm.

Not the clean kind.

Not the kind that asked you to rise instead of dissolve.

But Nina offered it anyway. She didn't cradle me. She constructed the scaffolding I could climb back up on.

Nina and Michael helped me—but not with softness. She handed me logic. Offered structure. Took me on walks. Brought me to the beach. Michael gave me small tasks around the house, took me out with his friends to local restaurants.

I tried to stay out of the way. I worried I was too much for them. That they didn't understand the depth of my pain. That I didn't know how to ask for help, because I didn't know what I needed.

Still, I continued to work. My job was remote already—based out of Washington, D.C. When I told them I'd be staying in Massachusetts for a while, they didn't blink.

They were wonderfully accommodating. Said, "Take the time you need." So, I tried. I kept to my routine as best I could.

Walked Shadow in the mornings. Poured my coffee in a white mug.

Opened my laptop like it might hold my life together. Worked. Breathed. Spent time with Shadow—just her and me, like it used to be.

And in the spaces between spreadsheets and silence,

I tried to remember what staying felt like.

Michael and Nina didn't ask questions. They just made space.

THE HAMMER AND THE ECHO

"You're free," she said. Hammer-voiced.
But the dark passenger whispered,
"Then why do you still feel owned?"
Freedom without feeling is a ghost town.

Thanksgiving came. A full table. A real one. Kindness baked into every dish. Warmth seated at every chair. My brother visited. I'd been thinking that week how guilt had a flavor- like cold metal and burnt toast. But that night, laughter returned like an old hymn. Even Shadow's guiltless grin was a balm. The dark passenger slinked back into the shadows, bored.

Hours before the guests arrived, Shadow and Miley got into the cooked turkey. Most of it, gone. Shadow and Miley were unapologetic. No panic. No yelling. Nina and Michael calmly sent me to get another turkey. We didn't say a word to the guests. But I remember. I laugh about that day sometimes.

THE FEAST BEFORE FORGIVENESS

Two dogs. One bird. No evidence.
Just laughter under candlelight.
A story we'll never tell the guests.
But I remember.
Because that night, guilt didn't sit at the table with me.

I told Nina and Michael that Marianne and I were going to

give it another go. They were skeptical. Eliza was skeptical. My parents too. But I was running out of money to pay the lawyer, and Marianne swore she'd changed. Michael said, "I don't think it's going to work. But I get it. It's a means to an end."

Nina said, "Fine. But she's not welcome in this house. Not for Thanksgiving. Not for Christmas. Not ever"

Christmas came. I spent it with Nina and Michael, and the rest of my family. Marianne didn't understand. I told her the truth: "They don't like what you did to me."

She hated it.

But Nina kept checking in. One day, she invited me to the mall. "Let's walk. Get steps in." She asked how Marianne was.

I told her, "She's trying."

And for a while, I believed it.

Until the knife danced. Shadow had stayed close that night. She watched Marianne leave the room, and then laid down at the door, not asleep- alert. When I curled up on the couch, she came up and pressed against me like ballast.

The dark passenger coiled but said nothing. Not even he could compete with her silence.

I called Nina the day after. I told her I needed her.

She didn't hesitate.

She became the shield I never knew I needed.

THE SHIELD SHE BECAME

She didn't weep. She didn't whisper.
She braced. She blocked. She bore the weight.
And when the dark came back,
She stood between it and me.

When I went to the hospital in March of 2024, my mom and Nina showed up at the ER. No emotion. Just a simple, "Are you okay?" That was her way.

After the ward, after McLean, she took me to pickleball. Said, "You're going to be okay."

And somehow, I believed her.

She hosted dinners, gatherings, summer barbecues.

She helped me survive the aftermath. Before my lease at my apartment expired in 2024, she bought a duplex and remodeled both sides. My brother lives in one unit. I live in the other. She gave me a home again.

THE HOUSE SHE BUILT
Not of wood. Not of siding.
But of second chances and floors that didn't collapse.
A place with doors that didn't slam,
And walls that remembered how to hold.
She gave me more than shelter.
She gave me a beginning.

She didn't hug me when I moved in. Just handed me the key. And I didn't cry.

But something inside me unclenched. She didn't coddle me. But she didn't leave. And when I needed her to be the wall that stood between me and the collapse—she was.

Nina gave me a place to rebuild. But Shadow—Shadow gave me the courage to stay rebuilt.

She and Nina never said much to each other, but I once caught them watching the same horizon from the porch. One with her arms crossed, the other with her ears perked. They were nothing alike. But they both stood between me and the fall.

For the first time in years, I wasn't looking for the exit. I was looking at the horizon they both faced. Nina with her arms crossed, Shadow with her ears pricked. Their silence wasn't empty. It was a perimeter, a place where my panic couldn't reach. Between them I started to practice breathing without bracing. Not healed. Not whole. But held

In that moment, the dark passenger didn't dare speak. Not when the two sentinels stood side by side. One made of blood, the other made of bone and bark. I was held by both.

THE TWO WHO STOOD
One barked. One didn't.
One questioned. One simply watched.
They didn't agree. They didn't need to.
They both held the line.

Silence meant different things between them. Nina's silence was loaded—made of logistics, questions she didn't need to ask, decisions already made. Shadow's silence was something else. More ancient. More alive.

When they stood on opposite ends of the same room, I could almost hear the dark passenger pacing—muttering, measuring. But he didn't speak. Not when they were both watching.

THE SENTINELS
Some walls are made of fur. Some of bone.
Some of sisters who don't cry in public
but still make sure you have a second helping of everything.

Nina didn't hug much.

Didn't say much.

But she came when I was drowning. She came without question.

And she stayed.

THE NIGHT THE WALLS HELD
Some sisters bring blankets.
Some bring weapons.
She brought both

23

THE ONES WHO WAITED

One gave me the map. The other taught me to walk. They built my spine with hands of opposite heat— One soft with rain, one stiff with stone. And both stayed. Through the flood.

THEY BUILT ME LIKE A CATHEDRAL. My father carved the stone. My mother whispered the prayers. And when I started to collapse, neither left the doorway.

I was always closer to my mom than my dad. Not because one loved me more. They both loved me the same—but spoke different dialects of devotion.

My mom was the empath. The social worker. The soft breath in the storm who asked, "How do you feel?" and then, "How do you feel about that feeling?" She believed healing was a spiral, not a straight line. She sent chakra meditation links, lit incense for clarity, talked about regenerative energy and breath work.

It always made her feel like she was helping. And it's the thought that counts—but things like that weren't what I needed. It was too touchy-feely for me. Sometimes I needed pragmatism.

Other times, I just needed silence. But when my world broke, I think she forgot her own philosophy.

When I started to heal, part of her wanted me fixed yesterday. I think it was her guilt and anguish talking—watching her kid suffer and feeling helpless.

My dad in contrast, when I started the process of healing, was more terse. He wanted me fixed yesterday too—maybe because he couldn't stand to see me in pain, but he framed it differently. It felt like he was telling me I had to get better for my mom, because she was suffering. And I caught myself wondering: then who am I healing for? Them—or me? I was walking a tightrope, trying to be vulnerable enough to seek help, but strong enough not to let them see how much it still hurt. Even when I shut down. Even when I couldn't answer. She stayed anyway.

My dad was pragmatic. Doctor by training. Structured, silent, composed. He believed in evidence. In strategy. In lectures dressed as care. When I brought him my pain, he gave me paths—not hugs. But he meant well too. He sent memes. Checked in. He stayed, just from a few feet further back.

THE ALCHEMIST AND THE ARCHITECT

One held the match.
One built the frame.
Neither knew how to stop the fire.
But they made sure I had a place to rebuild.

He wasn't there for the ward. Not because he didn't care, but because Mom understood the terrain of the mind better. He showed up where he could—packing boxes, carrying furniture, helping me rebuild a body that felt broken.

He was the one who bought my first guitar. Taught me the notes. Came to my soccer games and stayed just long enough not to make me nervous. When I fell off my bike and broke my wrist, I didn't tell him for two days. When I did, he reacted like I was dying.

"Why didn't you say anything?" he asked.

"I thought it'd get better," I shrugged.

"You fractured it in two places."

He shook his head and sat back down, quiet, steadying. He didn't lecture that time.

I think I've only seen him cry once. We were living in Ghana when his mother—my grandmother—came to visit us from Bolivia. After she returned home, she passed away from malaria. He stood in the kitchen when he got the news, holding the phone like it might break. He cried, just once, quietly. I don't remember seeing him cry since.

I remember standing in the kitchen, pleading to sleep over at my friend's house. Just for one night.

"You have your own bed," my dad said without looking up.

My mom softened beside him. "Fine," she said finally, "but we're picking you up early."

The next morning, at 7 a.m. sharp, they were at the door. I never asked again.

Not because I didn't want to.

But because I got tired of the battle—of having to earn something as simple as time with friends.

I got tired of feeling like joy was always conditional. Like I had to bargain for belonging.

And when I finally did get to go, it was always on their terms —early pickups, quiet disapproval, the subtle undercurrent of guilt that followed me home.

I hated leaving while everyone else stayed.

They'd still be laughing, still making pancakes, still planning what to do next.

And I'd already be gone.

I started choosing silence over disappointment.

Withdrawal over negotiation.

I don't know why it was always so hard for them to let me go —just to be a kid among kids.

Maybe there was something I didn't know.

Maybe they saw a fragility in me I hadn't named yet.

Once in a while, I still bring it up to my mom.

"Why did Nina get to go to sleepovers, have friends over, host movie nights?" I ask.

She always brings up the same story.

"The time we left the country when you were in fifth grade," she says. "You stayed with your friend's family for the whole week."

It's her go-to answer.

Their version of closure.

But it doesn't answer the question.

Not really.

It's always been that way.

I ask why, and they offer evidence.

I tell them how it made me feel, and they remind me what they did once.

It's their way of responding—proof instead of presence.

But deep down, I don't think they have the answers either.

THE HOUSE THAT MOVED
Some homes don't sit still.
They stretch across continents, carried in the bones of those who raise you.
Their walls may change, but the heartbeat stays.

In Ecuador, I learned to swim and ride a bike. In Ashland, I helped plant tulips with my mom. My dad and I mulched the flower beds. I still remember the smell—earth and sweat and spring. I helped him mow the lawn, rake leaves in the fall, and shovel snow in the winter. It was a rite of passage. I still remember getting lectured —lovingly—about how to use the snowblower. "Careful where you aim the chute," he'd say. "If you point it at the bay window, it could crack the glass." I used to think it was common sense—until years later, when I was in Oman, I got a call from my mom. She was furious. My dad had been snow blowing the walkway and kept the chute pointed the wrong way. A rock had flown straight through the bay window, right in the middle of a New England winter.

There was a time I thought Ashland would be forever. That I'd graduate with my friends. That I'd have the typical American high school arc—senior prom, yearbook signatures, summer goodbyes. Then they told me my mom got a job as Country Director for a project in Bolivia. That meant moving again. That meant breaking the rhythm I'd just started to love.

I remember asking if I could stay—if I could live with our neighbor and finish school in Ashland. I kicked. I begged. But the decision was made. I understood later that it was what was best for the family. But I never got to graduate with my friends. I never got closure. And for a while, I resented them for that.

To this day, a small part of me wishes I'd stayed.

"You'll thank us one day," my dad said as he zipped the last suitcase. "You just don't see the whole picture yet."

Maybe he was right. But at the time, all I saw was the fracture.

When we first moved to Ashland, I didn't belong. I didn't have words like "autism" or "masking."

Only that I felt wrong. Too much. Too quiet. Too weird. Too loud. But even that began to fade.

Things settled. Slowly, I found my rhythm. The codes became familiar—when to laugh, when to nod, how to disappear just enough to be liked but not noticed. And once the mask in America fit better, I started to have what felt like a normal life.

In retrospect, Ashland was the best move they ever made for me. It gave me something I hadn't had before: a version of *belonging*.

Even if they were still protective—about sleepovers, friends, independence—it was different.

Manageable.

I found joy here.

I loved it.

But when we moved to Bolivia, I stopped believing I had any say in my life. I became the kid who packed when told, smiled when asked, and disappeared when it got too hard. They showed up. They stayed. But sometimes I needed more than presence. Sometimes I needed them to see what I wouldn't say. And they couldn't. Not because they didn't care. But because I was good at hiding. And maybe they were tired of looking.

When I failed out of Landmark, they were furious. Rightfully. But they didn't abandon me. They helped me reset. Reapply. Recover. When I succeeded, they stood quietly behind me, proud but never boastful.

And then came the hardest goodbye for all of us. The house.

Ashland. The only place that almost felt like permanence.

The three of us stood in the driveway. Marianne, my mom, and I. My dad couldn't make it—he was working in Angola at the time. And honestly, that was a bit of a blessing. My dad's a bit of a hoarder—it's like he grew up during the Great Depression or something. We used the chance to do a clean sweep.

There was so much junk he kept. We filled two full containers. My mom focused on the essentials. We boxed them carefully and moved them to a storage unit, like a time capsule of our family's root system.

"Let's get the tape," my mom said, already organizing boxes.

I wandered inside. Every room was a ghost. My childhood bike leaned against the garage wall. The green door hadn't been repainted ever, but I drove by once. it's purple now. We sealed the flowerpots like time capsules, roots still clinging to soil they didn't know they'd lose.

I remember looking back and whispering, "Thank you." Not to the house. To them. My childhood flashed by—the summers of mischief with my sister, the clatter of my first band, the awkward joy of growing into myself. That house had been my anchor in a drifting world. I thanked them for giving me that—for giving me a place that held my shape, even after I left it.

That night, I stared at myself in the mirror. I looked older, sharper, like the boy inside had already packed and gone. My eyes didn't ask questions anymore. They just waited for orders.

THE ROOT THAT BLEEDS
Not all grief howls.
Some just echoes through the walls you once touched.
Some whispers follow you across oceans.
Some doors stay closed. Some—stay open.

Years later, when I told them I was pursuing an autism diagnosis, they hesitated.

"I don't think that's what's going on," my mom said. "Marianne's just... overdoing it."

When it came back positive, she blinked. My dad said nothing. Later, he sent a picture of a cat riding a Roomba. I didn't know what it meant. Maybe he didn't either. But he stayed in the chat.

THE DARK PASSENGER HIDES
He kept them from seeing.
Not because they didn't look
But because I learned to vanish.
And they mistook the mask for my skin.

We don't talk about the suicide attempts. My dad doesn't bring it up. He acts as if he doesn't know. I'm sure he does.

My mom does. Maybe she told him. But we don't speak of it —not because they don't care, but because we come from a lineage where feelings are whispered, not named. Still, they stayed.

During the false reconciliation in December, my dad came from Ecuador to help Marianne and I move into the apartment.

My mom didn't come—she didn't want to see Marianne at all. When my lease was up at that complex months later, my dad returned again to help me pack and move into the duplex. He flew across continents just to make sure I wasn't alone.

They live in Ecuador now. Cumbayá, just outside Quito. My mom the flower child, it's only fitting she moved into a neighborhood with that name. All she needs is a guitar, fire, and some people to sing the song with. Then there's my dad with the structure. They're five minutes from my sister's house. Grandparents now. Still lovers of the road. Still global nomads.

We talk almost every day. FaceTime, WhatsApp, or calls. The connection never broke. Even when I did.

They aren't perfect. But they're the kind of imperfect that matters. The kind that shows up with casseroles, lectures, hugs, and logistical spreadsheets. They gave me a life of movement. Of meaning. Of roots that grew sideways across continents.

THE LETTER I NEVER WROTE
I should've told you I was drowning.
I should've told you I was gone.
But you threw the rope anyway.
And waited until I came up for air.

They taught me to be kind. To work hard. To be honest. To respect everyone.

After my time at the ward, my mom asked how I felt. My dad asked what I planned to do next. Between the two of them, I learned how to spiral and how to survive. My mom lit incense and talked about regenerative energy and healing through breath. My dad preferred spreadsheets and silent car rides. One thought my autism was a gift I hadn't unwrapped yet. The other didn't mention it at all.

When I was younger, they were overprotective. Especially with me. Nina, on the other hand, had more freedom—parties at the house, boyfriends could come over even. I had to beg just to go to a sleepover. I think they sensed something fragile in me that they couldn't name. So they tried to shield it instead.

Nina seemed to move through the world without resistance. I learned how to stay quiet, how to self-correct, how to mask before I even had the language for it. I don't blame them. But I noticed. I still do.

THE MEMORY THAT STAYED

The house is gone. The street is older.
But the boy who lived there still hums down the hallway.
Some rooms echo louder than others.
And some never stop singing.
They gave me warmth.
I carried it like a torch.
Sometimes it burned me.
But it lit the way back home.

One Christmas when we lived in Bolivia, I learned what that kindness really meant. I don't remember what presents they bought me that year. What I remember is what they gave away. We spent the week before Christmas walking through town, inviting homeless and orphaned kids to join us for dinner.

On Christmas Eve, they sat at our table like family. We cooked for them, laughed with them, and gave them gifts. That moment—the warmth, the grace, the dignity of it—has never left me. That was the real gift.

They taught me that love doesn't always sound like "I love you." Sometimes it sounds like "I bought your ticket," or "Here is a meme," or "Let's go for a walk."

THE ONES WHO STAYED

They didn't shout. They didn't shine.
They just kept the porch light on.

I don't know how to thank them. I don't know if I ever can.

But I'll spend the rest of my life trying. When I brush my teeth and catch my reflection in the mirror, I see them both. My father's steadiness in the set of my jaw. My mother's fire in my eyes. I am what they built—through conflict, through silence, through casseroles and lectures and porch lights left on too long.

I never said thank you at the right time. I wish I had. But I think they heard it anyway—each time I kept breathing.

THE REASON I STAYED

I was fire once. I was ash once.
But they were the root.
And roots don't run from flame.
They deepen.
And they wait for rain.

Sometimes I wonder what the world will feel like when they're gone. When no more WhatsApp messages come through. When the porch light finally goes out. One day, I'll walk past a house and feel it—like a phantom limb. Their absence will echo in the spaces where their rituals used to be. I try not to think about it. But some loves are so deep they hurt in advance.

THE BLOOD THAT BURNS

I carry their flame.
Sometimes it scorches. Sometimes it saves.
But it is mine now.
And I will not put it out.
They weren't just the ones who stayed.
They were the reason I stayed, too.

They couldn't always see what I wouldn't show. But they stayed anyway. And maybe that was the truest kind of love.

I carry them now. Not just in the lines on my face, or the way I pace when I'm nervous. But in the way I wait at the window for the ones I love to return. In the way I leave lights on without thinking.

Last week, my dad texted me a picture of a dog wearing glasses. No caption. Just the image. The kind of quiet gesture that said more than words. A contrast to my mom, who digs for the roots. He left breadcrumbs. Together, they held me in their own languages. And somehow—it felt like home.

My mom called me the next day and asked how I felt. And how I felt about what I felt. It was classic her—circling emotion like a hawk, trying to pin it down with words. She'd always been that way, overanalyzing feelings until they frayed at the edges. I knew it came from care. But sometimes, I can't keep up with her questions. I shut down at the first part of the question. I always shut down at the first part of the question.

And somehow—it feels like home.

They didn't just stay. They stayed long enough for me to learn how to.

And now I stay for others. I stay for the broken boy inside me.

I stay because they did.

I'm still learning how to stay—for others. For myself.

The porch light is still on. I think I'll leave it that way a little longer.

THE LIGHT THAT STAYED

Not all love rescues.
Some just waits at the border of your grief,
Holds a flashlight,
And leaves the door cracked open.

24

THE REPRISE

Every story ends with a door. Some are slammed. Some drift open.
And some—some are still burning when you walk through.

THE COFFEE POT CLICKS. I brace like it's a bomb. It isn't. But some mornings, everything is. Shadow stirs beside the couch, her breath ragged, her nails tapping the floor like Morse code from the underworld. The sunlight creeps across the wood floor like it's afraid to touch me.

They say it's quiet now—but this quiet still has teeth. The kind that nibbles behind the ribs before they bite. I haven't crossed the threshold of this day yet. I hover in the doorway, waiting for some part of me to step first. And yet, I'm still here. The walls don't echo anymore. They absorb.

They remember.

THE FIRST BREATH
The survivor does not rise to applause.
He rises in fragments, unsure if the war ever ended.
The gods remain silent—not out of cruelty, but curiosity.

I count blessings like I used to count exit routes—carefully, suspiciously. Ava's laugh. Jenny's voice on the phone. My brother's teasing, disguised as affection. The small sacreds. And still—there are mornings I hold my coffee like a shield. I don't know where to set it down. Where to set *me* down.

Ava's gone now. But I still visit her like she's just late, not lost. I water her flowers at her gravesite. I drink coffee beside her name.

I tell her what Shadow's been up to. Tell her dad jokes I think she'd roll her eyes at.

Sometimes I laugh. Sometimes I just sit and wait. I wait for the silence to shift. For the air to crack just slightly. I don't bring prayers. I bring presence.

And I listen—not for words, but for the echo of someone who once held me without needing to fix me. Someone who saw the wreckage and stayed anyway.

THE FAULT LINE

The wounded hero fears softness more than steel.
Love once wore a kind face and tasted like ash.
He learned to duck even when no one was swinging.

My body remembers siege. Even in silence, it prepares. Shadow groans as she rises, her hind legs folding like tired scaffolding. She leans into me—not for help, but to remind me I still exist.

She's been there across oceans. Through vows and breakdowns. On the night I almost didn't make it, she didn't bark. She didn't run. She stood between me and the void like an oath.

THE DOG WHO STOOD BETWEEN

Some beasts do not guard the gates. They are the gates.
She saw the death approaching and lay across the doorway.
And death, confused, passed by.

She's not a pet. She's the last witness. The threshold guardian. The one who stands between who I was and who I might still become. And when the dark came, she didn't bark—she held the door closed until I was ready to walk back through it.

At night, when the house forgets our names, Shadow makes a patrol of the perimeter and returns to place one paw across my ankle. A weight the size of a promise. The dark passenger sighs like a bored god. She doesn't argue with him. She outlasts him.

The ghost arrives in fragments. A wine cork in a drawer. A hair tie beneath the radiator. The sharp click of the thermostat shutting off just as the warmth begins to settle into my bones.

Marianne's ghost doesn't scream. She seeps.

THE GHOST IN THE STORM

She doesn't haunt rooms. She haunts weather.
A barometric pressure drop in the gut.
The hush before thunder and the scent of wet regret.

I hate that I still feel her. But I like that it still hurts. Because pain, at least, is honest.

This house groans like something ancient learning how to breathe again. It creaks not because it's old, but because it remembers. It is settling. So am I.

Healing isn't victory. It's truce. Temporary. Tender. Conditional.

Ava once laughed at a stupid pun I made. I laughed back. Harder than I should have. That night, alone in bed, it felt like betrayal. Laughter tastes sweet in the mouth. Bitter in the gut.

THE SPLIT TONGUE

Laughter is the traitor's language.
A sound that once meant safety, now used in shadows.
Joy is a blade with no hilt.

So I practice with both hands. A joke dropped like a pebble into the day. A smile I don't apologize for. I let the sweetness cut the tongue and the bitterness teach me where I'm still thin. I don't throw the blade away. I learn how to set it down without bleeding.

I laugh. And I grieve. At the same time. The body can't always tell which is which. Steam clears the mirror. I brace for the face, like I'm peering through the veil between two worlds. My breath fogs the glass again before I can see. My eyes look bloodshot. A week-old stubble cuts across my jaw. Sometimes I see the boy who stood in the basement with nothing left. Sometimes—I see me, standing in the doorway between then and now, daring myself to step through.

THE SECOND GLANCE
The mirror isn't a reflection. It's a prophecy.
It shows who you might become—if you survive yourself.

The mirror doesn't bargain. It doesn't grade on effort. It offers terms: keep breathing and I will keep telling the truth. Some mornings the truth is a bruise. Some mornings it's a door. Both are honest. Both can be walked through.

One day, I bumped into my friend Brian's wife at a coffee shop. She asked how I was doing. I smiled. "Better." She believed me. I almost did, too.

But better doesn't mean whole. It means bleeding slower. It means screaming less audibly. One morning, I burned my toast again. Shadow gave me a look like I'd betrayed her faith and breakfast. The kitchen smelled like failure and something almost comforting.

SMOKE AND SALVATION
Reinvention is not sterile.
It reeks. Of charred memories and half-built selves.
The phoenix doesn't rise clean. He rises scorched.

Now that I'm still here, I'm becoming someone new. Not better. But *truer*.

And now, war. Not of violence—but reclamation. I lace my shoes like armor. Practice kindness like it's a form of battle. I beat shovels into swords and go looking for the places that need clearing.

Marianne still lives nearby. Close enough to find me if she wanted to. Sometimes I picture us in the produce aisle. Aisle five. Pears.

What would I say?

"I wasn't perfect. But I loved you. I fought to build something that didn't hurt. I failed. You hurt me. And I forgive you. Not because you deserve it. Because I do."

FALL, GOLIATH

The giant falls not from might—but from truth.
A pebble of clarity. A slingshot of release.
Down he goes, and the silence is sacred.

Forgiveness is not a halo. It's a hinge. It lets the door swing on something sturdier than rage. The room on the other side isn't brighter. It's just wider. I can stand up in it without hitting my head.

I return to the mirror. This time—on purpose. I stand in the doorway of my reflection. The dark passenger is behind my eyes, still watching. But he no longer holds the knob. I step through. I don't look away.

To Jenny, who told me I didn't have to earn breath. To Nina, who didn't flinch. To my brother, who stood still when I couldn't. To Ava, who saw me. To Shadow, who never asked for anything but gave me everything. To my parents, who didn't always understand but never stopped showing up—who held the door open even when I shut it.

To Eliza, who taught me how to sit in the fire without becoming it—who handed me the map back when I couldn't remember I had hands. Who never tried to fix me—only reminded me I was never broken to begin with. She didn't give me light. She gave me something better—a fire-lit map, still smoking at the edges. Maps don't rescue anyone. They refuse to lie. The ink won't move for you. You have to move for it. I folded the paper until the route touched my ribs and walked the line like a tightrope across the old fire.

I didn't follow it because I trusted the trail. I followed it because it was warm. Each of you stood at a different threshold and waited. You didn't push. You didn't pull. You stayed until I walked through.

THE ONES WHO STAYED
No hero survives alone. The myth is a lie.
Behind every sword lifted—
hands held, hearts broke, and someone stayed.

There's something I never said. I still miss Marianne. Not her the person, but *the her I built from scraps.* A fantasy stitched from loneliness and belief. A ghost of my own making. A god I prayed to so I wouldn't have to leave.

Sometimes, I still reach for her in sleep.

THE HAUNTING THAT HEALS
Some ghosts don't chain us. They cradle.
They don't say 'boo.' They say, 'breathe.'
And when they vanish, they leave behind
the shape of something we can grow into.
I didn't think I'd live this long
I didn't think I'd want to
I didn't think breath would feel like defiance
but here I am and it counts.

Now that I'm still here—I still hear echoes from the old life. The hand dryer at Target. The shivering cold of the basement floor. The way the hallway in the psych ward smelled like disinfectant and secrets. The white doesn't bother me anymore.

Once, the white was indictment. Now it's primer. The wall wasn't erasing me. It was waiting. I press my palm to it and leave heat instead of apology. The room accepts the print like a signature.

THE RETURNED

He left a boy, came back with ash on his skin.
They call it healing.
He calls it learning to walk without armor.

I opened the fridge one night and stared at the antifreeze bottle that was right next to the pantry. Not long. Just long enough. Shadow nudged me. Her claws clicked against the wood floor like slow thunder. The overhead light buzzed—too bright, too quiet.

The smell of coolant made my throat close. I dropped the keys. That was the night the mirror stopped being a stranger and started becoming a gate.

The house creaks. But it doesn't scare me now. I know the language of its bones.

Now that I'm still here... I stare the dark passenger down and pour my coffee anyway.

Now that I'm still here... I look at texts I never deleted and choose not to reach out.

Now that I'm still here... I press play on the voicemail Ava left me a week before she went to the hospital. I let myself cry without shame. Later that night, I stare at the ceiling and wonder what it would feel like to disappear again. Not die. Just dissolve. Just... go. The thought doesn't last long. But it visits. That's the thing about ghosts. They know the way back.

THE DARK PASSENGER SPEAKS

"You thought I was here to kill you," he says.
"But I was trying to keep you company when no one else would.
You hated me because I stayed.
But I was the only one who could."

He's quieter now. Not gone. But no longer clawing the wheel. He knows I can drive.

Go to the mirror. Not later. Now. Don't flinch. Don't fix your hair. Don't soften your face. Hold your own gaze like it's a spell. Because it is.

If he's still behind your eyes, like he is behind mine—let him see you. Let him *know* you walked through the fire.

And when you do—don't close the door behind you. Leave it open. For whoever is still crawling through the smoke.

Because now that I'm still here, I don't just breathe. This wasn't a reprise. It was a resurrection disguised as one.

I sing. Even if the song still cracks.

And the dark passenger—he doesn't haunt me now. He hums along.

The mirror is clean. The door is open. The breath? Still here.

Come in. I left the light on. If you're crawling, keep crawling. If your breath still fogs the mirror—you're not done. The door is cracked. The light is real.

And I think I will.

THE OPEN DOOR

It doesn't promise safety.
It offers passage.
Bring your breath. Bring your ash.
Leave the armor in the hall.
If your hands are shaking, good.
They'll ring the bell for you.

AFTERWORD

This is not an ending.

It's a threshold.

If you've made it this far, you've carried my ghosts with me—page by page, breath by reluctant breath. You've walked through the ash and ruin, through collapse and silence. And still, you stayed.

I didn't write this as testimony or spectacle. I wrote it because survival left me no other choice. Because the words in me had to find air, or they would have drowned me.

I am not fixed. I am not finished. But I am still here. And maybe that is the only miracle that matters.

Healing has no clock. No straight line. No finish date circled in red. Some tides recede quickly, leaving calm behind. Others drag you under again and again until you think you'll never surface. One never knows.

But if you are in the tide—ride it. Whether the storm is brief or endless, stay in the fight. Breathe when you can. Rest when you must. Rise when you're able. And know this: every moment you endure is defiance.

And to you, my friend, if the dark has taught you my language, I want you to hear this clearly:

You do not have to earn your right to breathe.
You are not too broken to stay.
Your stillness is not absence.
It is proof.

If you're struggling, that's okay. It sucks, I know. But say something. Reach out to 988. Talk to someone you trust. There's no shame in going to some place like McLean for a week to get more intense help. Be proud you're showing up for yourself. Because you matter. And the world is better with you in it.

IF TODAY IS HEAVY
If all you can do is not disappear, that counts.
If all you can do is drink water, that counts.
If all you can do is text "still here," that counts.
If all you can do is lie on the floor and let the dog keep watch, that counts.
The bar is not high. The bar is honest.

We are not alone in this. We never were.
And now, neither are you.

BENEDICTION FOR THE ORDINARY
May your keys jingle like proof.
May your mug be heavy enough to anchor you.
May your shoes remember the road back.
May the mirror hold your gaze without demanding a performance.
May the door you leave open be found by someone who needs it.

ACKNOWLEDGEMENTS

There are a thousand ways to come undone. Some loud. Some silent. Some so slow you don't notice until you're already gone. I didn't think I'd survive writing this. I didn't think I'd survive living it. But here it is. And here I am.

This book is stitched from breath I nearly lost, held together by people who didn't ask for perfection—only presence. People who met me in the wreckage and said, *You're still here. That's enough.* This is for them.

My beloved sister

For the one who came for me when the dark had already closed its fists.

For the one who turned headlights into a lifeline, who opened a door and did not flinch when I staggered through it.

You did not save me with speeches. You saved me with presence. With silence that was stronger than the voices tearing me apart. With action that asked nothing in return.

I know the cost. The weight you carried and never named. The way you built a shield out of your own bones and held it over me until I could breathe again.

This book is not just mine—it is ours. Because the night I would have vanished, you arrived. Because when I could not stand, you stood for me. Because I am still here, and the first reason is you.

Michael

For the man who never asked me to explain.

For the husband who opened his home to my ruins and never called them ruins.

You could have turned away. You could have asked why, or how long, or if I deserved it. You didn't. You just made room—at the table, on the couch, in the silence.

I know it wasn't easy. My storms didn't belong to you, but you weathered them anyway. You let me heal in your house without making me feel like an intruder. That kind of quiet strength is its own kind of mercy.

I carry gratitude for you in ways I don't always say out loud. But know this: your steadiness mattered. Your patience mattered. You mattered.

My mother

There were winters that lasted years. There were nights when silence pressed against my ribs like a verdict. But you—you were the hearth.

You didn't need to be loud. You didn't need to explain. You just stayed lit. Your quiet was never absence. It was *armor*. A kind of love that wrapped itself around me without demand or condition. You reminded me who I was even when I couldn't say my own name out loud. I could still feel your warmth.

You didn't ask for thanks. You never needed a spotlight. But the fire you lit in me still burns, even now. Even when I forget.

This is for the warmth that stayed when I couldn't.

My father

You were the mountain I pushed against, full of fury and misunderstanding. I didn't know I'd someday need the very stillness I once resented.

You taught me how to endure—before I knew that word meant more than surviving. You showed me how to stand when nothing around you made sense. You didn't offer many words. But you didn't have to. Your silence was a kind of foundation. It didn't bend. It didn't boast. It just *held*.

When the storm came, I leaned on you more than you'll ever know.

This is for the strength that stood still, and never cracked.

My brother

You didn't ask for explanations. You didn't demand recovery.

You just let me exist. Angry. Silent. Fractured.

You stayed in the room when most people left.

That was your magic—loving without commentary. Showing up without expectation. I didn't have to earn your presence. I didn't have to apologize for who I was.

You were just *there*. And that was enough.

This is for the quiet strength that never flinched when I unraveled.

Shadow

You didn't speak. You didn't have to. You *knew*.

When I couldn't tell the difference between survival and surrender, you stood between me and the threshold. Your eyes didn't just witness—they *refused*. You were the last line of defense when I couldn't see where the dark ended.

You didn't bark. You didn't run. You *stood*.

And death, confused, passed us both.

You are more than a dog. You are the only creature who saw every version of me—shattered, masked, silent—and *chose to stay anyway*.

This is for the kind of love that walks on four legs and breathes like a storm.

Eliza

You didn't promise me healing. You promised me space.

You never tried to fix me—you let me fall apart on my own terms, with someone watching. Someone who didn't look away. You were mirror, anchor, map. You reminded me that healing isn't linear. It's sacred. It's slow. It's brutal. And sometimes, it's *quiet*.

When the world made me feel like too much, you helped me find the version of myself that was *enough*.

This is for the voice that helped me name the dark without letting it own me.

Lauren

You gave me back my name. You reminded me that I was more than survival. More than the mask. More than the bruises no one saw. You made me laugh again—really laugh, the kind that shakes something loose in your ribs.

With pickles and playlists and poems, you cracked the old script. You made the air lighter. And so did I. You didn't try to erase the pain. You just held space for joy to *sneak back in*. This is for the day you said *stay*—and I finally did.

Katie

You didn't arrive to rescue me. You arrived to see me.

And you did.

You looked at the wreckage I'd become and didn't flinch. You laughed like thunder and loved like scripture. You never asked for perfection—you just asked for truth. Even when it was messy. Even when it hurt.

You showed me that love could still live in the aftermath. That a body with scars could still be beautiful. That the broken things didn't need fixing to be *holy*.

You kissed the parts I tried to hide, and called them sacred.

I will carry you in every line I write, every room I survive.

This is for the ghost who became grace.

Yvette

You met this manuscript in its rawest form—jagged, trembling, bleeding between the lines. You didn't turn away.

You helped me sharpen the blade without cutting the truth. You didn't try to smooth it. You didn't tame it. You let it howl. You let it burn.

You held the mirror when I was afraid to look. And what came back wasn't shame—it was *story*.

This is for the clarity you gave the chaos.

And the courage to speak it.

And to the ones who stayed

You didn't ask me to be whole. You didn't hand me a timeline. You didn't run when the mask fell.

You just stayed.

You waited in the dark with your hand out, not to pull me—but to remind me I wasn't alone.

You held the line when I vanished.

You whispered *stay* when I forgot how.

You didn't love the healed version of me.

You loved the one who was still burning.

So I stayed.

This book is not a victory lap. It's a resurrection. Stitched from the breath I almost surrendered. Forged by hands that didn't let go. Written in the language of those who stayed long enough for me to choose life.

If there is light in these pages, it's because you kept the match burning until I could hold it again.

This is for you—the sacred few. The unflinching. The fire keepers. The ones who waited for my return.

I'm still here. And because of you—I *chose* to be.

ABOUT THE AUTHOR

 **Christopher Carazas** is a third culture kid, trauma survivor, and social impact strategist who grew up between languages, continents, and expectations. Raised between Bolivia and the U.S., in churches that preached grace and families that didn't understand neurodivergence, Chris learned early that survival meant performance. He became fluent in masking before he ever learned the word for it.

Diagnosed with autism as an adult, he spent years trying to function by disappearing—until the marriage collapsed, the dark passenger stirred, and the mask shattered under the weight of silence. Twice, he almost didn't make it.

Now That I'm Still Here is not a triumph narrative. It's a reckoning. A sacred autopsy. A love letter to the ones who feel too much, mask too well, and wonder if breath still counts after everything breaks. This is for the ones who stayed. Or wanted to.

Chris has led global social impact measurement efforts across four continents, helped rebuild communities in crisis, and spent long nights rebuilding himself one breath at a time. He believes grief can be holy, laughter can be armor, and that a German Shepherd named Shadow once stood between him and the void like a myth made of fur.

He now lives in Kingston, Massachusetts, where the ghosts are softer, the silence is no longer a weapon, and healing walks beside him—slowly, imperfectly, but still moving forward. You can find more of his writing—memoir fragments, poetic hauntings, and sacred truths—at **substack.com/@ccarazas**.